The middle years of this century marked a particularly intense time of crisis and change in European society. During this period (1930-1950), a broad intellectual and spiritual movement arose within the European Catholic community, largely in response to the secularism that lay at the core of the crisis. The movement drew inspiration from earlier theologians and philosophers such as Möhler, Newman, Gardeil, Rousselot, and Blondel, as well as from men of letters like Charles Péguy and Paul Claudel.

The group of academic theologians included in the movement extended into Belgium and Germany, in the work of men like Emile Mersch, Dom Odo Casel, Romano Guardini, and Karl Adam. But above all the theological activity during this period centered in France. Led principally by the Jesuits at Fourviére and the Dominicans at Le Saulchoir, the French revival included many of the greatest names in twentieth-century Catholic thought: Henri de Lubac, Jean Daniélou, Yves Congar, Marie-Dominique Chenu, Louis Bouyer, and, in association, Hans Urs von Balthasar.

It is not true — as subsequent folklore has it — that those theologians represented any sort of self-conscious "school": indeed, the differences among them, for example, between Fourviére and Saulchoir, were important. At the same time, most of them were united in the double conviction that theology had to speak to the present situation, and that the condition for doing so faithfully lay in a recovery of the Church's past. In other words, they saw clearly that the first step in what later came to be known as *aggiornamento* had to be *ressourcement* — a rediscovery of the riches of the whole of the Church's two-thousand-year tradition. According to de Lubac, for example, all of his own works as well as the entire *Sources chrétiennes* collection are based on the presupposition that "the renewal of Christian vitality is linked at least partially to a renewed exploration of the periods and of the works where the Christian tradition is expressed with particular intensity."

In sum, for the *ressourcement* theologians theology involved a "return to the sources" of Christian faith, for the purpose of drawing out the meaning and significance of these sources for the critical questions of our time. What these theologians sought was a spiritual and intellectual communion with Christianity in its most vital moments as transmitted to us in its classic texts, a communion that would nourish, invigorate, and rejuvenate twentieth-century Catholicism.

The *ressourcement* movement bore great fruit in the documents of the Second Vatican Council and has deeply influenced the work of Pope John Paul II and Cardinal Joseph Ratzinger, Prefect of the Sacred Congregation of the Doctrine of the Faith.

The present series is rooted in this twentieth-century renewal of theology, above all as the renewal is carried in the spirit of de Lubac and von Balthasar. In keeping with that spirit, the series understands *ressourcement* as revitalization: a return to the sources, for the purpose of developing a theology that will truly meet the challenges of our time. Some of the features of the series, then, will be:

- a return to classical (patristic-mediaeval) sources;
- a renewed interpretation of St. Thomas;
- a dialogue with the major movements and thinkers of the twentieth century, with particular attention to problems associated with the Enlightenment, modernity, liberalism.

The series will publish out-of-print or as yet untranslated studies by earlier authors associated with the *ressourcement* movement. The series also plans to publish works by contemporary authors sharing in the aim and spirit of this earlier movement. This will include interpretations of de Lubac and von Balthasar and, more generally, any works in theology, philosophy, history, literature, and the arts which give renewed expression to an authentic Catholic sensibility.

The editor of the Ressourcement series, David L. Schindler, is Gagnon Professor of Fundamental Theology at the John Paul II Institute in Washington, D.C., and editor of the North American edition of *Communio: International Catholic Review,* a federation of journals in thirteen countries founded in Europe in 1972 by Hans Urs von Balthasar, Jean Daniélou, Henri de Lubac, Joseph Ratzinger, and others.

RESSOURCEMENT:
RETRIEVAL AND RENEWAL IN CATHOLIC THOUGHT

available

Mysterium Paschale
by Hans Urs von Balthasar

The Letter on Apologetics *and* History and Dogma
by Maurice Blondel

Prayer: The Mission of the Church
Jean Daniélou

Letters from Lake Como:
Explorations in Technology and the Human Race
by Romano Guardini

The Portal of the Mystery of Hope
Charles Péguy

In the Beginning:
A Catholic Understanding of the Story of Creation and the Fall
by Cardinal Joseph Ratzinger

Hans Urs von Balthasar: A Theological Style
by Angelo Scola

forthcoming

The Discovery of God
Henri de Lubac

PRAYER

The Mission of the Church

JEAN DANIÉLOU

Translated by
David Louis Schindler, Jr.

WILLIAM B. EERDMANS PUBLISHING COMPANY
GRAND RAPIDS, MICHIGAN

Originally published as
Contemplation: Croissanie de L'Eglise
© 1977 Fayard, Paris

English translation © 1996
Wm. B. Eerdmans Publishing Co.
255 Jefferson Ave. S.E., Grand Rapids, Michigan 49503
All rights reserved

Printed in the United States of America

01 00 99 98 97 96   7 6 5 4 3 2 1

Library of Congress Cataloging-in-Publication Data

Daniélou, Jean.
[Contemplation. English]
Prayer : the mission of the Church / Jean Daniélou.
p.   cm. — (Ressourcement)
Includes bibliographical references.
ISBN 0-8028-4105-8
1. Spiritual life — Catholic Church.   2. Catholic Church — Doctrines.
I. Title.   II. Series: Ressourcement (Grand Rapids, Mich.)
BX2350.2D317513   1996
248.3 — dc20   96-9103
CIP

Contents

Foreword, by Hans Urs von Balthasar   xi

Introduction   xv

PART ONE
THE PRIMACY OF GOD

1. The Meaning of God and Adoration   3
   - I. God as the Supreme Reality   3
   - II. God's Presence to Humankind in Jesus Christ   6
   - III. Being Present to God in Prayer   9

2. Prayer   11
   - I. Prayer as an Expression of Religion   11
   - II. Prayer and the Presence of the Trinity in Us   18

3. "Lord, Teach Us to Pray the *Our Father*"   21
   - I. The Conditions of Prayer   22
   - II. The Contents of the *Our Father*   23

CONTENTS

PART TWO
ADVENT AND HOPE

1. Advent   31
   I. The Meaning of the Word *Advent*   32
   II. The Notion of Advent in the Old Testament   33
   III. The Different Times of Advent   40

2. Hope   42
   I. The Foundation of Hope   43
   II. Hope Assumes the Orientation of Our Being
       toward Its Spiritual Fulfillment   46
   III. Hope Means Patience   50

3. Missionary Hope in the Old Testament   54
   I. The Theme of the New Jerusalem   54
   II. A Commentary on Isaiah 60   57

PART THREE
THE MYSTERIES OF CHRIST THE REDEEMER

1. The Mystery of Christ and the
   Three Times of Advent   67
   I. The Waiting in the Old Testament Is Fulfilled
      in Christ   68
   II. The Second Advent and the Time of the Church   72
   III. The Third Advent: Christ's Return   75

2. The Evangelical Spirit of Humility   76
   I. The Humility of the Sinner   78
   II. The Humility of the Creature   79
   III. The Humility of Christ   82

Contents

3. Redemption: The Center of the Trinitarian Plan   85

   I. The Preexistence of God's Plan in the Love of the Father   86

   II. The Accomplishment of God's Plan by the Blood of Christ   89

   III. The Action of the Holy Spirit   91

PART FOUR
THE GROWTH OF THE CHURCH

1. The Spirit of Mission   95

   I. The Foundations of the Spirit of Mission   95

   II. Concrete Expressions of the Spirit of Mission   103

2. The Apostle's Mission as a Continuation of the Mystery of Christ   107

   I. The Incarnation   108

   II. Participation in Redemption   110

   III. Pointing toward the Resurrection   113

3. The Mission of the Holy Spirit   115

   I. "The River of Living Water Flowed from the Throne of God and the Lamb"   115

   II. The Spirit Descends upon the City   118

   III. The Spirit's Actions in Our Lives   121

Foreword

Anyone who knew the author, or rather narrator, of this book as well as I did — for years we shared a desk in a theology classroom and would often secretly read the Fathers during boring lectures — will find him living again in each of these short chapters. Others will be delighted with the rich diversity of his ideas and the accessibility of his language, though they may be somewhat disconcerted by the sudden changes of points of view and by the apparent untidiness in the layout — until, that is, the inner form of this extraordinary man becomes real before their eyes. Then they will realize that they are standing before a fountain that constantly shoots up and pours forth on all sides. In fact, they are really under a waterfall, the power and plenitude of which they sense, without being able to grasp.

In purely human terms, Daniélou was a bundle of energy, like quicksilver, open to any challenge: an idea; a new plan; but still more, a fellow human being, especially when the person concerned was in spiritual need. He was a self-consuming flame, ready to burn himself up for some project which fascinated him and to which he would dedicate himself with incredible concentration for a couple of months, or for one of the countless areas of his apostolate. Day or night he found time for people of every kind: for the members of his *Cercle Saint-Jean Baptiste,* which was concerned with dialogue with other religions and cultures (especially Islam); for philosophers, writers, and artists; and also for those dubious circles that he entered with Parzival-like naturalness — he never shunned contact with them — and that brought him so much vicious calumny at the time of his death.

During his years as a cardinal, he succeeded with great resolution in continuing his scholarly work, producing book after book on the Fathers, Philo, Jewish-Christian theology, aspects of the Old Testament, Qumran, and, above all, on the great perspectives of the Christian theology of history. The collection of his brilliant reviews (in *Recherches de Science Religieuse*) on all the literature he was following remains perhaps his most important achievement. Meanwhile, he found time not only for his teaching and administrative duties at the Institut Catholique, but also, almost every evening, for discussion with groups of students and academics, with people of every religion and level of education. This passionate enthusiasm for the cause of Jesus Christ and the Church of Rome and her great tradition, this unhesitating and prodigal generosity, explains a great deal about Daniélou: the occasionally somewhat unfinished quality of his scholarly works (despite the clear intuition of their basic themes); the long-term effects of his apparently wasted apostolate; the hatred and contempt for him from some Church circles (not to mention the similar treatment he received from within his own religious order); and, finally, his premature death, which leaves a gap that cannot be filled.

He loved. He loved not only God and the central mysteries of the faith, but also everything he praises in this book. He loved prayer and was deeply convinced of its "political," world-transforming efficacy. He loved humility, which he radiated, and poverty, which marked his life even as a cardinal, so much so that it provoked amazement in people wrapped up in decorum. In his apostolate in the Church, he loved to work as Church beyond the Church and to send out sparks in the Holy Spirit.

When seen as a whole, the following talks, which were given at days of recollection for the laity, follow a clear path: from the encounter with the living God, whom we are allowed to call "Father," (I) to the presuppositions of that encounter in salvation history; from the Old Testament, whose structure of hope is still valid for us, (II) to the encounter with the mystery of redemption in the New Testament; (III) and from there to existence in the Holy Spirit in the Church (IV). There is clearly a Trinitarian structure here, in line with both biblical and patristic thought. But then, in each section, the speaker is overwhelmed by an abundance of different points of view. Everything is interrelated, because one cannot talk about the Father except in the Son and through the Holy Spirit. The Old Testament cannot be discussed without its orientation toward the New. One cannot speak of prayer without referring to action, of Christian ideals without keeping in view the crude and tragic realities of the sinful world and Church.

Every great matter of concern surfaces somewhere in Daniélou's scholarly work — the most profound, of course, appearing the most frequently. First, there is the natural religiosity of humankind, which, according to Catholic doctrine, is the indispensable presupposition for all revelation of grace. On this basis, he calls always for popular religion — instead of a religion of elites and closed groups. From here, the conversation begins with all the non-Christian religions, not least Judaism, which remains for him, in a very Pauline way, the "holy root" from which Christianity came forth. In addition to the ever-present ecumenical horizon (which never misled him into blurring what is distinctively Catholic), the movement of his thought is always forward. However, while this forward movement was seen and interpreted by Teilhard de Chardin in strongly evolutionary and scientific terms, it is first and foremost biblical for Daniélou. The Old Testament is hope for messianic fulfillment, a hope that is indeed fulfilled in the person of Christ, though it continues to exist in his body, the Church, as she is built up through the centuries until the final perfection of the cosmos. It is not for nothing that the term *Advent,* in all its phases, is central to his view of history.

FOREWORD

The reader will be convinced of the truth of what is said here, and admit that many seemingly simply worded sentences are, in fact, genuine pearls of wisdom. Without being pedantic, I should like to place this whole book under the motto coined by the author himself: "There is no difference between contemplation and mission. It would be absurd to have to choose between the two. Mission is nothing other than the self-unfolding of contemplation."

Hans Urs von Balthasar

Introduction

Prayer is a time of contemplation and silence in a setting that helps us to disengage ourselves from life's immediate concerns. It is an opportunity to live more closely to God, to dwell in his presence, and to nourish ourselves with his Word. The goal of prayer is not to seek ecstatic experiences; rather, it is to discover something profound, something substantial, something that fortifies our faith and animates our zeal for souls. In this sense, each person prays for him- or herself, because prayer is first the soul's encounter with God.

On the other hand, it is also an opportunity to recall our responsibilities before the Church and to ascertain better how to fulfill them. In this sense, prayer bears on the problems of the Church in the world and what part we must take in them.

Preliminary Remarks

Prayer, which is an essential aspect of Christian life, is an immense realm. We have only just begun to explore its mysteries. We often have little taste for prayer because we are not sure exactly what it is. And yet, prayer is one of the principal dimensions of our lives and our eternities. To be occupied with God is the highest occupation. But this requires an apprenticeship.

To penetrate God's word in the Bible or in the liturgy, to contemplate nature, or to reread the Psalms, trying to discover God in a personal way — these are all ways of putting ourselves in a prayerful disposition. And that is the one thing that matters.

The tragedy of the modern world is that it no longer occupies itself with God. One of our essential reasons for existing, therefore, is precisely to give witness to adoration, to give God the place in our own lives that the world denies him. We too easily forget what ought to be the primary focus of our spiritual life. As La Pira has imaginatively put it, "the world rests on two pillars: contemplative monasteries and workers' barracks." In other words, there are two fundamental dimensions to existence: the love of the poor, the abandoned, the disinherited; and the gesture that carries us spontaneously toward all suffering, the practice of adoration.

We must therefore accustom ourselves to this double rhythm of adoration and service, which together form a complete existence. I would thus deny that a life dedicated exclusively to service would truly be a human existence. To affirm the central place of adoration, which many people feel, but are ashamed to admit, is one of the Christian's *raison d'êtres* with respect to others who often do much more in the realm of service than we are able. Not every Christian is required to be a mystic, but all Christians — even those who are just learning to pray, those for whom meditation is something difficult — must be persuaded that prayer is essential in the order of values, and they must be prepared to make a minimum of sacrifices so that prayer can have a real place in their lives.

PART ONE

The Primacy of God

CHAPTER ONE

The Meaning of God and Adoration

I. God as the Supreme Reality

God is the supreme reality; he is what is most important because he is what is most real. Through a radical error of judgment, most people attach importance to secondary things, failing to recognize this absolute primacy of God.

The Old Testament, by contrast, is pregnant with the intensity of divine realities. Here, the creature appears in his nothingness; and God, in his supreme reality. Things are set aright:

I love you, Yahweh, my strength!
Yahweh, my rock, my fortress, my deliverer,
my God, my rock of refuge.

Yahweh thundered from the heavens,
the Most High gave forth his voice:
hail and burning coals!

He reached out and grasped me,
he drew me out of the deep waters.

3

Yahweh rewarded me according to my justice;
according to the cleanliness of my hands he requited me.

[Ps. 18:1-2a, 16, 20]

All of these simple images clearly express the intense reality of God. Consider also certain phrases from the prophets or from mystics. "No one can see the face of God and live," Moses says (Exod. 33:20), which means that God's existence is so intense that we find it intolerable: our flesh is not able to bear it; it devours us; it terrifies us. We often worry that God's weight would be to heavy for us, so we avoid contemplating him. God seems to be too demanding, and that is why some of us avoid thinking about him.

God's marvels inspire Job to say: "these are but the outlines of his ways, and how faint is the word we hear, but who could endure the thunder of his power?" (Job 26:14). Thus, we may already find the beauty of the world unbearable at times; how much more unbearable it would be if the very Creator of this beauty were to manifest himself!

God's glory, which Moses found unbearable, moved St. John of the Cross to say that "God is Darkness," precisely because his light is so brilliant that it burns our eyes. And Rilke, in a poem, writes these remarkable lines: "If one of them [an angel] took me suddenly upon his heart, I would succumb to death from his overwhelming existence, because beauty is nothing but the beginning of terror." The presence of God disconcerts and disorients us so much that it arouses in us a holy fear. In his book on the majesty of God, Hans Urs von Balthasar develops the idea that beauty is but the reflection of divine glory: that which sometimes overwhelms us in the beauty of certain symphonies or of certain landscapes is just a manifestation of the reality of divine glory, the brilliant radiance of God such as he is in himself.

We have a tendency, as St. Augustine would say, to stop ourselves at these traces of God that hide their creator from us instead of leading us to him. Everything speaks to us of God because we live in a world that comes entirely from him. This universe of symbols

4

is such that, if our hearts were filled with God, we would see him in all things. Most of the time, however, the things that surround us become barriers between God and us and provide an occasion for sin, whether these things be material goods (food, clothing, the satisfaction of the senses); or other people, who arouse external reactions of sympathy or dislike, hostility or emotion; or our work, which absorbs us to such an extent that it ends by engulfing us. Now all of these things ought to lead us to God; and the spiritual life consists precisely in approaching God through all things, discovering God's presence in the ordinary aspects of our lives.

As St. Paul says, "In him we live and move and have our being" (Acts 17:28); and the psalmist: "If I go to the ends of the earth, I find him, and if I enter into the depths of my heart, I find him who is more interior to me than I am to myself."

"He is at once infinitely great and infinitely small," the Pseudo-Areopagite says magnificently, "the greatest and the most subtle, the most exterior and the most interior, the immutable and the source of all life." We cannot place God in any category because he is the fullness of all things. As for me, I am like a blind man immersed in light. Heaven is not somewhere else; though I am not aware of it, I live in the midst of paradise.

In a beautiful book on spirituality, *La théologie de la mystique,* Dom Stoltz explains that a mystic is a person who has returned to paradise. He is the new Adam; and the world, for him, is paradise. We may have this experience in those furtive moments when we feel reconciled with the whole of the universe and all who dwell in it. Such moments take the place of our more common experience of the world broken by sin. The extraordinary experience of the presence of God can and should be the normal atmosphere of our lives. During the times that it is, our relationships with our brothers and sisters reform themselves in the image of God; and we rediscover, through these relationships, the life of God that is their source.

II. God's Presence to Humankind in Jesus Christ

In Christ, God's proximity becomes infinitely greater. God comes to meet us in Christ and elevates us beyond ourselves so that we may penetrate his world, something that is difficult to achieve otherwise. In Christ, God's presence is infinitely more intense and infinitely nearer; in him, God invites us to enter into the very mystery of his own life. Through him, we become new creatures capable of dwelling in the intimacy of the triune God. To be Christian is to be open to God's gesture toward us, which introduces us into the very interior of his life.

These are basic Christian affirmations, and yet they often remain foreign to us. The first thing we learn as a child is the sign of the cross: in the name of the Father and of the Son and of the Holy Spirit; Mass is entirely addressed to the Father, through the Son, in the Spirit; baptism is given in the name of the Father, of the Son, and of the Spirit. Our whole Christian life is immersed in the life of the Three Persons, in the mystery of the love that exists eternally in God and in which we are called to participate through Christ. This is a *reality* that is given to us, and it is our duty to discover it as a reality and to allow it to penetrate ever more deeply into our lives. We have the responsibility of a whole Trinitarian education of our souls: we must learn to deal with God as we would a father; we must learn to allow Christ to pervade our lives so that we may become, like him, truly children of God; we must allow the Holy Spirit to form us inwardly, to govern us, and to guide our souls. Then, God would no longer appear to us as an overwhelming majesty, as an unbearable weight, such as he appears to pagan persons, people of the flesh to whom God is a stranger.

Christ is God, who has conformed himself to us so that we may become conformed to him, so that we may be empowered to understand, to love, and to experience the things of God. He renews our understanding so that we may comprehend what we otherwise cannot comprehend, and he renews our hearts so that we may love what we do not love naturally.

6

Prayer thus becomes, as Dom Marmion says, "the blossoming of our feelings that results from our divine adoption." It consists in developing the theological virtues, those new dispositions that result from the fact that we are children of God. For a Christian, to pray is to *make an act of faith, hope, and love.* Many of those who are baptized, who have in them the seed of the virtues, have never made an authentic act of personal faith; they have never come to trust absolutely in the Word of God. Why should we be surprised, then, if their faith is so fragile? Their faith is more of a wager than a total engagement of the understanding with respect to the Word of Christ. For Christ expects us to trust him totally; he expects us to take what he tells us seriously. Christ can act only in the situations in which he encounters faith: "He performed no miracles in Nazareth," the Gospel writers tell us, "because his brothers did not believe in him" (Matt. 13:58; Mark 6:5-6).

The most difficult theological virtue is hope. In spite of the promises of Christ, how many Christians there are who haven't the slightest certainty that they will one day enter into possession of the beatific vision and the overflowing joy of God! How many Christians there are who live without the conviction that they are moving toward this joy! And these people thus show little disposition to generosity because lacking certainty about what is to come, one would rather, as they say, get the most out of this life.

An act of faith, hope, or love is always a victory. In the same way, prayer consists in overcoming the bitterness and remorse that we often feel in the beginning of our meditation, by realizing that in God we possess all goods (which thus excludes any bitterness), and that Christ grants us his forgiveness and reconciles us completely with God (which thus excludes any sadness, remorse, or anxiety). Prayer is not at all a sentimental attitude or spiritual affectivity; rather, it is an inward confrontation and vanquishing of the flesh. So it is to the extent that we gain this victory in prayer that we become capable in the rest of our lives of putting things in their true place. In this sense, the object of prayer is the forming of the fundamental dispositions, which in turn permeate the rest of our lives.

7

Therefore, if we cannot acquire these dispositions in prayer, we will not have them in our lives.

A person who has learned to attain these visions of faith in prayer will be able to guide himself in life accordingly. But someone who has not trained himself thus will remain an unformed Christian. To the extent that the theological virtues train us in the various dispositions that come from being children of God, we gradually discover the precise, concrete realities to which this exercise of prayer corresponds: being children of God in Christ, we ought to deal with God as we would with a father who loves us. We are already the heirs of the kingdom, St. Paul says, which means that we already possess the divine treasures, even if we cannot yet enjoy them: "All that you ask of the Father in my name, he will grant you" (John 16:23).

This saying is absolutely just, not on the level of material goods (fortunately, for we would fall under the criticism that is often laid against us, that religion is motivated by self-interest), but on the level of love. What is essential is not what is given to us (God has revealed his attitude toward money, Pius XII said, by distributing temporal goods more or less haphazardly, as much to his friends as to his enemies), but what we do with what we are given; and God has committed himself to helping us succeed in love. The success of a life is determined by what it does with the materials given it. These materials always include some good things and some bad things, for every life contains both positive and negative elements. There are some people who are given all the materials needed and still fail; while there are others who are terribly poor (true poverty is not financial poverty but emotional poverty, a poverty in the limitation of gifts) and who, through this poverty, achieve a noble success: consider the lives of certain sick people who are nevertheless spiritual successes. A life has failed only when it has not been able to succeed in being what it could have been. The success of our lives depends on us, and God always grants it to us when we ask it of him. There is nothing more distressing and more false than to deny his help.

We thus see how prayer engages the depths of our being, and how it must help us to rediscover our spiritual vocation in all of its fullness and to rise above anything that might keep us from fulfilling it.

III. Being Present to God in Prayer

What is this rediscovery of God? What does it mean to be present to God in prayer?

To pray is first to discover what God is in himself and to wonder at it. Adoration means to awaken ourselves to the wonders of God, the *mirabilia Dei,* and to let them astonish and delight us. Mme. Lot-Borodine explains that this is the true gift of tears — not the miserable tears of vexation, nor the tears of repentance, but the tears that burst forth when the wonder that God is touches our hearts so deeply that it overwhelms us.

Secondly, there is the filial prayer in which we engage God as a Father who helps us in all our needs, with the certainty that he will grant everything essential. It is the prayer in which we feel that the Son of God helps us to enter into his own filial attitudes.

Finally, prayer is an entering into the ways of God, an acceptance of the divine plan that God carries out in the world. It means becoming aware of the God who is coming, and not simply of the God who is. If we were only aware of the God who is, we might have the feeling that prayer withdraws us from the movement of life, and that there is an opposition between the contemplative life and the movement of history. But this is quite false. The God who is, is also the God who is coming, and the entire world is the accomplishment of the plan that comes from God and is moving toward God.

One way of finding God is to try to enter into the meaning of that which he wishes to accomplish among us. We find God when we discover that we are with him as workers in a marvelous world, a world in which the body of Christ is forming, a world in which the word of God, through whom all things are uttered into existence, fulfills all things by his incarnation in order to lead them to their end. One way of finding God is to realize that our lives find their meaning to the extent that they are conformed to God's plan, to the extent that they come to understand themselves as vocation; that is, in the service of something that is truly worth our efforts. In this way, human realities and divine realities meet, because it is through human activities in themselves that we work toward the realization of God's plan.

That is why the Second Vatican Council, in seeking to express humankind's divine vocation, evokes the great principles of the family, the social order, international life, peace, and all the realities that, though they appear to be merely human, are fulfilled by the grace of God that brings them to completion. The call of Christ is at their source; they find their fulfillment in the supernatural beatitude of the Trinity, toward which we are all headed. In moving from the source to completion, we pass through the whole of human reality. The reason, then, for the diversity of vocations is so that the whole of this reality is brought to realize its end. There is certainly a way of finding God in his creative and effective activity in the world. We participate in it to the extent that we do our best to conform our lives, in their professional, familial, or intellectual dimensions, to the accomplishment of God's plan. Through this, we transform our lives into vocations, and this grants them an absolute value.

"One loses the desire to live when one refuses to order one's activity in relation to one's vocation." This is a very profound comment from a modern novel. We have only to see how that which makes up the reality of our lives relates to our vocation; we have only to hear the call God makes to us to work with him. Quite often it is not a matter of doing something different, but doing it differently.

CHAPTER TWO

Prayer

Prayer ought to be in our lives something as simple as our relationships with the ones we love, as natural as the air we breathe.

I. Prayer as an Expression of Religion

The word *religion* designates two things: on one hand, it means the various forms of ritual worship of God; on the other hand, it means the basis of adoration, by which we fulfill our obligations toward God. The latter is what is meant by the virtue of religion.

Prayer by itself has value as an objective act. In this sense, prayer fulfills a function of the Church. Monks have been entrusted by the Catholic Church to recite the Office, the *Opus Dei;* it is their way of fulfilling their function, whether they have the desire to or not, whether they experience consolation or desolation, just as an engineer must fulfill his function by operating machinery, whether he feels fit or not.

When we speak of prayer, we must eliminate any questions of inclination or temperament. It is discouraging to see how many people attach importance to these dispositions, when in fact they have no such importance. Considering prayer as a simple, potent

11

activity that a person must fulfill in order for his life to be complete eliminates a whole series of false questions about sincerity or insincerity.

Going to Mass when we feel nothing for God is not at all a form of hypocrisy — it is faith. To pray is not merely to experience God. To make the emotions the gauge of religion would end in many aberrations. This is true of all personal relationships: love is situated beyond our emotions, which does not, however, mean that we distrust them. Emotion means the wonderful experience of love through a certain harmony of being. Love, on the other hand, is the very fact of a communion established between two beings situated on a level that is more profound than the sphere of our feelings.

Sincerity does not consist in conforming our behavior to our spiritual states, but rather in maintaining our behavior in spite of our spiritual states, in maintaining our profound fidelities in spite of our superficial infidelities. To be sincere means to be faithful to that to which we have truly given our heart in the fullness of freedom. This is what ought to exist in marriage and in friendship, in spite of all the possible external vicissitudes. Loving God means knowing that we can count on God and that God can count on us in spite of our emotional complications. Referring to the theological virtues, Jacques Rivière once said that "faith means to believe in God in spite of appearances; charity, to love our brothers in spite of what they may do to us; hope, to hope for spiritual goods even when they seem to be impossible."

We must therefore protect the substance of prayer from the vicissitudes of our experience and from our religious feelings, because it is founded on something that lies beyond them: prayer is the expression of our fundamental relationship to God.

The diversity of the Church's functions within the unity of the body of Christ is something very beautiful. It is important that we hold to the task that is entrusted to us by the others: the apostle must concern himself with souls, the monk recite the Office, the nun care for the elderly. By not fulfilling our function, we betray the trust of all the others. A monk who would leave his monastery too

12

often, even for an authentic apostolate, would nevertheless be spiritually deluded, because the entire Church needs him to recite the divine Office. As St. Paul says, "If one member is sick, the whole body is sick" (1 Cor. 12:26).

The best way to love others is to fulfill our task well. There may, in fact, be ways of concerning ourselves with others that would be a betrayal of our function (for example, students who forsake their work in order to devote themselves to various activities). There are "virtuous" people who wear themselves out because they believe they are responsible for everything, something that creates a perpetual bad conscience. There are certain good outcomes that are not our responsibility, and we disobey God when we concern ourselves with them. The only absolute law is God's will for us. It is through God that we go toward others. It is in obeying him that we are faithful to our sisters and brothers, even if this implies certain external infidelities. We always cause someone pain when we want to please everyone; besides, this is not what it means to love.

One of the problems of the spiritual life is learning to remain stable in the face of false guilt in our personal relationships. Psychoanalysis has taught us much in this area. Of course, it is not always easy to discern what God asks of us. This is the problem of the exercise of freedom, the problem of selection, and of choices, in which a number of factors come into play. True sincerity, which we have said does not depend on our spiritual states, is a potent, free, and definitive fidelity, by which we engage ourselves in what we know is truly demanded of us. With respect to prayer, this is expressed in the fact that we set apart some time in our lives that God has asked us to give him, whether we feel like it or not. And this ought to be protected from our imagination, from our feelings, and from the vicissitudes of our emotions. It ought to be so integrated into our lives that it never comes into question, no matter what our psychological dispositions may be.

We pray in order to please God, not to please ourselves. Although prayer is essentially an act of love for God, it is possible to make it into a subtle form of self-seeking. Prayer is a means of bearing witness to God: by this act, which is sometimes difficult, we demonstrate to him that we prefer his will to our own. We give him the part of ourselves that belongs to him. And we bear witness to a greater love for him when we pray faithfully even in the times that we lack the desire to pray.

Two things matter in prayer: doing it, and allowing God to accomplish his work in us. Sometimes the Holy Spirit touches our hearts, truly converts us (when he sends such and such an obstacle, such and such an antipathy, when he makes us discover what humility is), and makes us feel what it is to love God. God gives us these movements from the Holy Spirit when he wishes, and they are essential because we know that they do not come from us.

This, then, is the basic difference between Christian prayer (because these movements from the Spirit are not the result of a technique) and Buddhist meditation, which is a technique ordered toward the exploration of the internal universe. Hinduism has come quite far in this order and is to be admired; for Hindus, the exploration of being is more interesting and more mysterious than the exploration of the cosmos. Nevertheless, Christian prayer is something entirely different: it is essentially being moved by the Other, establishing a communication of love between God and us that lies beyond any technique, because it is the nature of a person to transcend technique.

Moreover, spiritual enlightenment is not always tied to the times of prayer: Mary of the Incarnation remarked that her greatest revelations about the Holy Trinity were given to her while she was rolling barrels along the quay at Tours. Indeed, it is striking to see how many people, experiencing dryness in prayer, have received astonishing spiritual enlightenment during their other activities. This demonstrates the sovereign freedom of God's grace. But these people still must have been faithful to their times of prayer!

Prayer would, in fact, become suspect if it were too attached to a particular feeling. The great mystics were very wary of feelings. St. John of the Cross is almost too severe in this respect; St. Ignatius is more human and makes much of the spiritual consolations that aid us, but "spiritual indulgence" would be to seek in prayer more for personal satisfaction than to give God his due glory.

In our age, prayer is also a *battle,* a giving witness in a world where people tend to become closed up in themselves. Christians must bear witness to the transcendence of God in a world that threatens to die from spiritual suffocation. Even if they have to struggle, Christians must preserve this "window that opens into God's infinity."

Each one of us has the responsibility to determine the place of prayer in our lives. Humble prayers (such as those in the morning or at night) and vocal prayers have great value and are a way of glorifying God; so, too, is the life of the sacraments, which is essential, even when it becomes a burden for us. There are great sinners who continually fall into grave sin and who, because they do not want to abandon the Eucharist, accept the painful servitude of going to confession every eight or fifteen days so that they can go to communion. There are many, by contrast, who give up the faith because of their moral difficulties. This is regrettable, for it is not our difficulties in being Christian that discredit the truth of Christ. All things become threatened for the one who begins to stray from the sacraments. Being rooted in the faith is fundamental: "I will not leave Jesus Christ despite all the vicissitudes of my existence."

Prayer is the expression of an ontological bond that exists between God and us. It is the outward manifestation of a fundamental reality: we continuously receive ourselves from God, and we continuously refer back to him. This bond between God and us is so profound and intimate that we may see our existence as the unceasing gift that God makes of ourselves to ourselves. For a Christian, existence is a relationship between two beings. To exist is to be loved: "I exist only to the extent that I am loved." This is a startling revelation. Whatever difficulties the Christian may have in his or her relationships with other people, he or she is never alone. Dialogue is the basis of our existence, because dialogue is what is absolute: the Trinity is dialogue. Because of the relationship of persons that exists first in God, then between God and us, and finally among us, all things come down to the following three realities: God is love; God loves us (and we are in a relation of love with him); and, finally, we must love one another and lay down our lives for each other. If we base our lives on these realities, they acquire an infinite meaning; and whatever vicissitudes may arise, we will always be circumscribed by love.

When a Christian is confronted with atheism or with other religions, he or she must be convinced of these essential things in order to be able to explain them. A Christian must be able to say to the Muslim: for me, love is part of God's nature, in contrast to your lofty idea of God. This glorious revelation given to us in Christ does not take away any of God's overwhelming majesty; but it introduces us into the mystery of the divine relationship, which is the reciprocal gift among the three Persons.

Prayer is thus the expression of our basic relationship to God; from this perspective, it is a mode of being. There are atheists who are sincere people, but they nevertheless miss a dimension of being. Moreover, many of them feel this, which shows that there is something radically inhuman and incomplete in atheism. Formerly, it was Christians who had psychological complexes with respect to atheists; now it is atheists who are beginning to have complexes with respect to Christians! Though we do not have complexes, we must remain aware that there is a way of being Christian that would give us a complex: if our Christianity were only a feeling; if it were slavery to a tradition from which we dared not free ourselves, or slavery to rules that we dared not violate; if it were merely an emotional attachment to our memories of First Communion. If any of these be the case, then we must either abandon everything so that we can rediscover the faith some other way, or — and this would be preferable! — we must implement changes in ourselves and come to all of these things in the fullness of liberty.

Prayer is also an act of thanksgiving *(eucharistia):* a recognition that *"tout est grâce"* (all is gift). But it is also a *sacrificium;* that is, an act concerned with the sacred, an act for God. This is the reason for the existence of secular priests. The ritual sacrifice, which is the priest's office, is ordered toward the inward sacrifice, of which all Christians are ministers. In this, we offer ourselves to God as a living sacrifice, and we consecrate ourselves to him by preferring his will to our own. There is thus a continuity between the ritual sacrifice and the real one, between sacrament and sanctity. Both tend toward the same goal: that the sovereign goodness and divine kindness be recognized. In this sense, Christ appears as the paradigm of humanity, because he is the first human who has loved God the way God deserves to be loved. It is for this reason that in the sacrifice of the Mass, we offer up Christ's human love for God, which gave itself unto death, and which came to fulfill our poor loves, in order to offer them to God.

Thus the sacrament recapitulates the ontological structure of being. Philo of Alexandria says that in human history there have always been two types of people, two attitudes toward being. On one hand, there has been *philedia,* the temptation to refer everything to humans; on the other hand, there is the *eucharistia* who refers everything to God. Cain is the symbol of the first tendency; Abel, of the second. Today this is a collective and subtle temptation; instead of a selfish individualism, we have a collectivism that is at once an openness toward others and a rejection of God. Claudel's remark, that "you do not need God in order to do good," is terribly modern. What we once asked from God, we now ask from humanity. This is a subtle form of pride, a pride in doing the good, the belief that humankind is the source of goodness toward others. A self-sufficient humanism would be considered the most noble today. We believe ourselves capable of bringing salvation to the world through our own powers. And this kills the religious attitude at its roots.

Though we no longer live in a time of anti-clericalism, we nevertheless live in a time when humankind's relationship to God is being called into question. Atheists are more inclined to accept the Church than they are to accept God (something that ought to worry us); they see in the Church only the services that it renders to humanity, rather than the essential aspect of its mission: the witness that it first gives to God. And this is fundamental for us: the religious attest to this in one way, and we must attest to it as laypeople in the world.

Prayer becomes a battle in our lives because it runs at cross-currents with the habits of the world in which we live and which gives it less and less space. It is obstructed by both our professional work and our leisure, which risks being so organized that it no longer has any room for gratuity. Prayer, as something gratuitous, finds increasing difficulties in securing space for itself in our social and psychological lives. Still, prayer is a vital function, not only of the individual, but also of society. From this perspective, the Islamic culture possesses certain advantages that we don't share in Western civilization. Saying this does not imply, however, that we must establish some form of clericalism; but it does mean that the relation to God is a constitutive part of a total humanism. Let us once again recall La Pira's comment, "the true city is one in which men find their home, and God finds his." One who has this double aim possesses the complete vision. In their preoccupation with finding homes for men, people today have forgotten the house of God.[1]

II. Prayer and the Presence of the Trinity in Us

Prayer is a drawing near to the Holy Trinity dwelling in our souls. This is a fundamental supposition of Christian prayer; that is, it is no longer the prayer of a creature, but that of a child of God. Grace establishes a new relationship between God and us: "God lives in us and we in him" (1 John 4:15).

Several verses from John's Gospel express this extraordinary reciprocity: "Remain in me as I remain in you" (15:4). "We will come to him and make our dwelling with him (14:23).

The mystery of this "dwelling" is one of the great mysteries of the Old Testament.[2] God dwells in the midst of his people. *Dwelling* means a *continual presence* as a principle of intimacy and a whole

1. Cf. J. Daniélou, *L'Oraison, Problème politique* (Paris: Fayard, 1965).
2. J. Daniélou develops this theme in *Le Signe du Temple,* or *De la Présence de Dieu* (Paris: Gallimard, 1942).

dynamic of relationships. This mystery is fully expressed in Christ, in whom God dwells: "The Word was made flesh and dwelt among us" (John 1:14). He continues this dwelling in us, who are the "temples of the Spirit." That God dwells in the inaccessible depths of our soul is an incredible reality. This "dwelling" is not something physical, but rather it is the expression of a new relation of strict intimacy: the Trinity is the continuously vivifying principle in us that communicates the life of the Spirit to us. The presence of the Trinity in us is the presence of God in the cosmos. God's presence takes three forms: (1) the presence of God in the universe; (2) the presence of God in the Jewish people and in the temple of Jerusalem; and (3) the ultimate presence of the Trinity in Christ and in the members of his body, in the intimacy of our souls: "In him we live, and move, and have our being" (Acts 17:28).

Prayer thus consists in making ourselves present to him who is present to us. God is present to us, but we are absent to him. To pray is to become aware of his presence. Presence is much more a matter of being attentive than it is physical proximity; it is above all a spiritual act. Consider the absence of people who are physically present — in the metro, for example — and the presence of those we love who are absent, a presence that transcends even the boundaries of death. The Curé d'Ars speaks of an old peasant who would say about his prayer, "He advises me and I advise him"; and La Bruyère says, "When we are with the people we love, it makes no difference whether we talk to them or not." When two people who love each other are present to one another, just the fact of this reciprocal presence gratifies the heart. The instant that God is there, my heart is gratified. What more do I need? This is the silence of love.

In order to descend into the sanctuary of our souls, which are God's dwelling place, we must pass through three regions: the region of distractions, which is easy enough to get beyond; next, the region in which we discover ourselves with all of our good and bad feelings (we generally stop here, because this region is very difficult to pass through); and finally, the depths of ourselves, the region in which

19

the Trinity dwells, and into which we must do our best to descend directly, as a stone falls to the depths of the sea. This is the reason that prayer requires some practice. By praying, we discover these various obstacles, and we learn to find the concrete attitudes of prayer. Prayer cannot be achieved impromptu; regular practice is necessary.

CHAPTER THREE

"Lord, Teach Us to Pray *the* Our Father"

When the apostles ask Jesus, "teach us to pray," the Lord teaches them the *Our Father*, which remains the primary prayer of the Christian (cf. Matt. 6:10-13).

We have all known and recited the *Our Father* since our childhood. But can we ever claim to have understood it? Have we ever penetrated the meaning of its expressions that are so rich and, in certain respects, so disconcerting? For this reason, it is good to meditate on them. For meditation is a penetration into the meaning of things we already know — or, rather, things we think we know, but whose contents we are, in reality, far from having understood. If we were capable of saying the *Our Father*, giving each sentence its full meaning, we would know how to pray perfectly. Let us therefore try to deepen our understanding.

We will begin with some remarks on the general teachings that Christ gives about prayer when he comments on the *Our Father*. These comments have always formed the basis of the Church's teaching. In fact, in the early Christian communities, the preparation for baptism consisted of three initiations:

- an initiation into the faith, in which the candidates were taught the symbols;

21

- an initiation into the Christian life, in which they were taught the basic Christian mores;
- a formation in prayer, which was essentially Christ's comments on the *Our Father,* the very expression of Christian prayer.

I. The Conditions of Prayer

"When you pray, go into your room and pray in secret. And your Father who sees in secret will repay you" (Matt. 6:6).

Our Lord explains to us that our prayer must above all be something sincere, something done in God's presence, something done so that God alone sees it. Now, in our lives, we tend to attach more importance to what other people see than to what God sees. And yet true freedom and sincerity would be to act only for the sake of pleasing God, without concerning ourselves with what others may say or think. This frees our hearts from countless complications, duplicities, and contrivances, in which we taint what is authentic with an impure self-seeking and a false concern with how we appear in the eyes of others.

Our Lord also tells us not to multiply our words in prayer, because prayer is not some sort of magic formula: "As if they will be heard because of their many words" (Matt. 6:7).

Prayer consists, rather, in an interior attention and a conversion of the heart, because what turns us away from God and keeps us from praying is less the number of words than it is the number of desires or worries that preoccupy us. Precisely after the text of the *Our Father,* Our Lord says, "Do not worry about what you will eat or what you will drink" (Matt. 6:25). In this sense, the very condition of prayer is a certain quieting of our desires and regrets; that is, it is an act of interior detachment and of conversion, a self-surrender that disengages us from the things that drag us down and distort us, in order once again to open ourselves to God in the simplicity of our hearts.

II. The Contents of the *Our Father*

An excellent way to pray is to take a passage from the Gospels and to penetrate it inwardly. Let us try to do this with the phrase "Our Father, who art in heaven."

We recall the story of the peasant who was asked, "So what do you do when you pray?" He responded, "I simply say, 'Our Father, who art in heaven.'" His interlocuter remarked, "But you don't add 'Hallowed be thy name, thy kingdom come, etc.'?" And he responded, "When I say, 'Our Father, who art in heaven,' just these words fill my heart so much that I have no need to go further." There is no doubt that just one of the phrases of the *Pater Noster* would satisfy our hearts for a long time. To this end, let us discuss some of the characteristic elements of this first phrase.

The *Our Father* is a prayer, that is, a petition.

To pray is thus to make a request. This may perhaps surprise us; isn't prayer primarily adoration? Of course, praying is first adoration, that is, letting ourselves be overtaken by the splendor and beauty of God, and thus allowing that form of admiration which we call adoration arise within us. But to pray is also to make a request — not in the sense that prayer is self-interested, but that it is an expression of poverty.

We pray because we are poor in the sense in which the word *poor* is used in the Gospels: a poor person is one who is aware of being sick, destitute, and in the midst of suffering. Not to pray, then, would be a form of complacency and self-satisfaction, not being aware of our suffering. We need to be profoundly aware of our suffering, to feel how spiritually poor we are, how little we know God, how little we love him, how little we love our brothers. This is what our Lord meant when he said that he came, not for the just, but for sinners. The just are those who believe that they are what they ought to be, when in reality we are all sinners. With respect to this fundamental reality of sin, prayer is a cry that we utter to another. It is this that

23

defines every prayer. One begins to open oneself to God when, aware of one's impotence to deal with things on one's own, one turns to God for help; from this moment on, one is open to the work of grace.

Prayer is an act of humility; it is the humble prayer of those our Lord spoke about when he said, "Blessed be the poor in spirit, blessed be the humble, the kingdom of God belongs to them. Blessed are those who hunger and thirst . . . blessed are the persecuted . . ." (Matt. 5:3-10).

There are two sides of humanity, the rich and the poor. When we pray, we stand with the poor — with all the poor, both the materially poor and the spiritually poor. We allow humanity's anxious waiting for God to be expressed through us. All through the Gospels, we see that it is the poor people who are open to God.

The *Our Father* is a filial prayer.

The *Our Father* is the prayer of the Son who knows he is loved by the Father. We open up our hearts with all of our needs before the Father, knowing — because he has not only told us, but has also made manifest — that he loves us and that he wants to give us what we truly need. He knows what we need better than we do, and he is always ready to grant it to us.

The *Our Father* ought therefore to be a profoundly confident prayer: we offer to God all of our soul's needs; we should be capable of being ourselves, of admitting the things that most cause us to suffer: our personal failures, our inability to love, our inability to pray, all of the destitution we feel, our inability to achieve what we would like to for God's kingdom. As Léon Bloy said in *La Femme pauvre,* "there is only one thing that is sad: not to be a saint." We ought to feel Christ's love to such an extent that this sadness remains alive in our hearts as a sort of wound.

But we must express all of these sufferings in the knowledge that we are loved, and that therefore they do not present an obstacle for us. The Gospels are full of stories of those who are sick and who come to find Christ. We, too, are sick and are in need of healing. The ability to tell God everything we feel and everything we need is very comforting and very true; and at the same time, it places us in a state of humility and simplicity of heart.

When we address the Father in prayer, we do so as children of God. That is why, during Mass, we say the *Our Father* only after the great prayer of thanksgiving, which ends thus: "Through Him, with Him, and in Him, all glory and honor is yours, Almighty Father, forever and ever," and we continue: "In the words our Savior gave us" (cf. Matt. 6:10-13) "we dare to say. . . ." In other words, only the Son is able to refer to God as Father, and it is only to the extent that we are in him, with him, and through him that we are able to speak to God and behave toward him as children do toward their father. We do not have sufficient faith in this love that surrounds us, and our prayer is not confident enough. Whatever our sins may be, whatever our suffering may be, from the moment we turn to the love of the Father in confidence, all things cease to be an obstacle to our relationship with him.

Furthermore, the *Our Father* is a prayer that is certain of being heard, because everything that we ask for has already been won for us: participation in the spiritual goods, the spiritual success of our being, and all the things that have been given to us in Christ. For this reason, prayer does not consist in gaining what we do not yet have, but rather in entering into possession of its treasure. By this I mean that because we are children of God, we already own all of God's possessions. However, for many of us, this treasure lies within a sealed chest that we leave unopened; we do not enter into possession of the goods that actually belong to us. A Christian ought to be a person who is radiant with life, drawing from the treasures God has given, transfigured by charity, radiant with an unshakable faith, filled with such hope that life's difficulties never succeed in stifling his thirst for happiness.

What scandalizes unbelievers is that saying the things we say, we fail to live what we are: "We would believe if we felt that you really believed," they say, "but how do you expect us to believe if you give us so little impression of believing yourselves?"

There is thus, in the prayer of the *Our Father,* the certainty of being heard, because we are essentially asking God to bring to fruition those things for which we already possess the seed: his life, eternal life, and the spiritual fulfillment of our lives.

The *Our Father* is a collective prayer.

That we do not say "My Father" is of fundamental importance. There is nothing individualistic about the *Our Father:* it is a prayer in which we embrace all other people, a prayer that is at the same time an expression of love. We go to the Father only with our sisters and brothers. This is the counterpart to what we mentioned earlier, that we go to our sisters and brothers only through the Father. These two are reciprocal truths. Just as it is true that we are in union with our sisters and brothers only when we love them in God, so it is true that we do not truly go to God except when we go to him with all of the others.

In the *Our Father* we pray for the fulfillment of God's plan for all humanity; we enter in a certain way into God's own intentions when we ask that his will be done. It is thus a prayer that opens us to the entire world; and more specifically, it is a missionary prayer: from one end to the other, the *Our Father* includes the presence of those who do not know Christ, those who are in the midst of spiritual suffering. It is a prayer that bursts forth from a heart that suffers to see God so little known and so little loved, and that humbly expresses this suffering. It helps us to get beyond all selfishness and to love, in a disinterested way, the good of all mankind. Charity — indeed, love itself — means to desire the good of all people; and this is what the *Our Father* opens for us and teaches us.

It is for this reason that the greatest saints achieve perfect prayer through the *Our Father.* It is not at all an elementary prayer; it is at once the simplest and most profound of all the prayers.

The *Our Father* is a prayer of praise.

Finally, this prayer of request is a prayer of praise because its three requests, "hallowed be thy name, thy kingdom come, thy will be done," bring us to desire God's glory.

It is a prayer that speaks of God's love, a prayer that brings us to seek the extension of praise, which first presupposes that we ourselves are souls of praise, because it is to the extent that we love God that we suffer from his not being loved, that we desire for him to be loved, and that the wish that "his name be hallowed" takes on its full meaning. And, what is very important for us, it helps us to reach that mysterious point where adoration, contemplation, and mission coincide. Mission is the extension of adoration, because adoration means that we desire that God be known and loved by everyone and not just certain people.

May this brief commentary thus help us better to understand the meaning of the *Our Father.* We ask the Holy Spirit himself to instruct us in it. If, henceforward, we no longer recite the *Our Father* half-heartedly, but instead, if each request becomes charged with the meaning we have uncovered in these pages, it will have been an incomparable acquisition. Indeed, when a person has thus meditated upon and experienced a prayer, it takes on a completely different meaning when he or she recites it later.

When meditating, we must pause over the things that nourish our souls, without worrying about thinking over everything the preacher may have said, or everything we may have read. This would, in fact, be a form of distraction during our meditation. What is necessary is to pause at the things that move us, or, better, the things the Holy Spirit inspires in us, and to immerse ourselves in them until we have truly penetrated the text. According to St. Ignatius, what nourishes the soul is not the multiplication of words, but the inner experience of things. In the silence of our hearts, then, let us try to enter into this missionary prayer in which Christ brings us to embrace all the needs of humankind and of the world, and to offer them to the Father in the humble certainty that he will grant them.

PART TWO

Advent and Hope

CHAPTER ONE

Advent

The spirit of Advent is an attitude of waiting for the accomplishment of God's reign and for his coming in every nation. The notion of Advent is fundamental throughout the Bible.

In prayer, we must not only deepen certain spiritual attitudes but also affirm our convictions. For it is convictions that order our choices, and we occupy ourselves only with the things of which we are convinced. We lack not courage or will, but rather a deep conviction that would drive our courage. Indeed, the resources of courage and even heroism that even the laziest of people exhibit when they desire something are extraordinary. What strikes us about our age is precisely the lack of deep convictions. Goodwill is abundant, but because it has no solid foundations, the subsequent choices are not made. Hence, we find an exaggerated impressionability that puts itself at the mercy of every influence and calls into question what ought to be firmly established. This state of impressionability is proper to adolescence; but if it continues, it betokens immaturity. We must realize that the ability to choose is no small matter, and must devote ourselves to it in earnest.

In speaking of Advent, we begin with the conviction of an existing order, which then brings us into the domain of faith; for faith is a faith in the word of God, and the word of God is essentially a promise. Christ has promised us the salvation that he has brought to the world. Do we really believe what he has told us?

I. The Meaning of the Word *Advent*

The word *Advent (Adventus),* meaning "coming," is the Latin translation of the Greek word *parousia.* To talk about Advent implies that someone or something is coming or will come.

The liturgical time of Advent is a waiting for divine action, a waiting for God's gesture toward us. We wait with the Old Testament, St. John the Baptist, and the Blessed Virgin in preparation for the coming of Christ.

The Letter to the Romans expresses in an extraordinary way the fact that the whole of creation is in a state of waiting: "Creation waits with eager expectation for the revelation of the children of God" (8:19). We live in the last stages of this waiting, which means that we still live in a time of Advent, but in a cosmic Advent that encompasses the whole of creation.

Advent is not only the waiting for an event, but also the waiting for a person. These ultimately come to mean the same thing, because the awaited event is precisely God's intervention in history: the coming of Christ, the Son of God. That is why the Bible generally expresses this waiting in the form of a waiting for the person of Christ, as the one sent by God. The book of Revelation thus ends with this sentence: "The one who gives this testimony says, 'Yes, I am coming soon.' Amen! Come, Lord Jesus" (Rev. 22:20). And the Letter to the Corinthians quotes this same phrase in Aramaic: *"Marana tha"* (1 Cor. 16:22).

Apparently, the phrase *Marana tha* ("Come, Lord") was one of the most common prayers of the early Christians. This attests to the fact that their basic attitude was one of waiting for the definitive return of Christ. The Christian does not have to break free from time in order to enter eternity (as the Hindus do), but is rather required to assume a state of waiting for the entry of eternity into time and to take up the actual movement of history, which itself awaits its fulfillment in God's intervention. Christian prayer does not consist in escaping from, but rather in committing ourselves to, the ultimate end of the world.

"He who is coming" is the very name of Christ. We use it during Mass in a particularly striking text: "Holy, Holy, Holy Lord, God of power and might," bringing us to feel the abyss that separates us from God. We continue: "Blessed is he who comes in the name of the Lord!"

We could say that there are two moments in the religious attitude: the first, in which we become aware of our suffering and how infinitely far God is from us in his majesty, holiness, and grandeur; and the second, in which we come to see that the abyss that is insurmountable for humankind has been overcome by "he who comes in the name of the Lord." The claims of all forms of gnosticism — whether of the mystics, the Greeks, the Indians, or any other — to take hold of God's transcendence are inconceivable for us. The transcendent God would be inaccessible unless he were to give himself to us. Christ represents God's gesture of love, which comes to find us in order to bring us to him. He assumes our flesh and grabs hold of each of us in order to introduce us into the house of his Father, to fill us with his Spirit, and to lead us into the inaccessible world of the Blessed Trinity. This gesture on God's part is the object of our contemplation, and it expresses itself in our attitude of waiting.

II. The Notion of Advent in the Old Testament[1]

We will discuss three successive aspects of Advent in the Old Testament: the promise, the prophecy, and the figure of St. John the Baptist.

---

1. The themes sketched here are developed further in the following works by Jean Daniélou: *Le Mystère du Salut des Nations* (Paris: Ed. du Seuil, 1946); *Le Mystère de l'Avent* (Paris: Ed. du Seuil, 1948).

Abraham and the Promise

The notion of Advent in the Old Testament appears with the promise made to Abraham. Abraham is mentioned in the canon of the Mass (the sacrifice of Abraham), and he holds a significant place in the thought of St. Paul, for whom he represents the model of faith. He is the first to have received and believed in the promise: "Go forth from the land of your kinsfolk and from your father's house to a land that I will show you. I will make of you a great nation, and I will bless you and make your name great. You will be a blessing: I will bless those who bless you and curse those who curse you. All the communities on earth will find their blessing in you" (Gen. 12:1-3).

The author of the Letter to the Hebrews applies this text to Jesus Christ, saying, "it is by faith that Abraham, in obedience to God's call, went out to a place that he was to receive as an inheritance, and set out without knowing where he was going" (Heb. 11:8).

All of the work of St. John of the Cross is contained in this. Faith is not based on experience, which is always limited and discouraging, but on the promise; in other words, faith means to believe in things that we have not experienced. It means to set out, at God's word, for an unexplored country, for the inheritance that God has promised us: participation in his life. To give us this, God needs only our faith; and faith is tied neither to our aptitudes, nor to our talents, nor to our temperament. Faith provides the aptitude of itself.

The contrast between Socrates, or salvation through self-knowledge, and Abraham, or salvation through the promise, is a common theme in contemporary philosophy. Abraham is a man who has received God's promise, a man who sets out because of this promise, and who bases his entire life on the word of God. A text from Häring clearly demonstrates the difference between the pagan tendency and the Christian attitude: "The Christian is not a princess who has been exiled and who wishes to return to her country, but rather Abraham, who sets out for an unknown country which God will reveal to him." The choice is decisive: not a nostalgia for the past, or a return to the source, but a departure toward something new and unknown. We all have a pagan inclination, that nostalgia for past experiences and perfect moments. There are many (including Proust) who consider the perfect to be something behind them; and faced with the passing of time that mars and ruins, the only thing left for them is to recover the paradise of childhood. This is the tendency of the *Grand Meaulnes* and of poetry in general.

Abraham surmounts all of this. He is someone for whom the Promised Land is something yet to come. He takes leave of his country, his family, and the house of his father; that is, of all that is familiar to him. He will never again return to Ur, in Chaldea. For him, it is an irreversible departure; time is something meaningful. There is no sort of facile optimism here, but rather a certitude based upon God's promise. This is the whole of the Christian life: we are heading toward paradise, toward the unknown: "Unless you become like little children, you will not enter into the kingdom of heaven" (Matt. 18:3). God works great things in the one who believes. Consider what a great sinner Augustine had been, and how he was entirely renewed because he believed. "Behold, I make all things new" (Rev. 21:5). It is the nature of God's power to renew, to re-create, to reconcile what was separate, to remake the covenant, to free what was held captive, and to heal what was sick.

The Prophets

The promise made to Abraham is renewed with the prophets, who both testify that God kept his word in the past and announce that we are heading toward another Promised Land, of which the first was only a prefiguration. What God has already accomplished for his people is nothing next to what he will accomplish in the future.

Let us consider the example of Isaiah (43:16 and following), which repeats the canticle of Moses. Note how, in this respect, the Bible meditates continually on the same themes: Exodus recounts for us the flight from Egypt, the Prophetic Books return to this episode in order to develop it further, and the New Testament includes a reflection on Abraham and Easter. In this sense, we could say that Revelation comes down to a small handful of simple and basic ideas that we must penetrate to their depths because they form the keys to understanding everything else. "Remember not the events of the past, and do not consider the things of long ago. Behold, I am going to perform new wonders!" (Isa. 43:18-19, and following).

In the future, God is going to make things even more miraculous than the springs that burst forth from deserts. These will be "springs of living water." John tells us that this water is the Spirit, who will spring forth in the desert, from a chosen people, making their way toward paradise (John 4:14).

The things of long ago were indeed great (nothing in the Bible is ever disparaged); but we pass from miracle to miracle, or as St. Paul says, "from glory to glory." This, according to the Bible, is the constant law of existence; its implications are of fundamental importance for the spiritual life. We must not stop at any particular stage, but continually move on to what is ahead.

Our understanding of time is one of the most important things in life: if we are held captive to the past, either by what was good or bad, if we are branded by our failures, if we believe that our sins cannot be redeemed, if we are slaves of memory in the face of the mystery of death, we follow the pagan inclination in our being. We must, in opposition to this, react by faith. This same faith of Abraham, which is renewed again in us, allows us to overcome the past and respond to the call of the Spirit.

One who truly believes that the love of others and the service of God passes from miracle to miracle, and who accepts the successive deaths and renunciations that are included in this, is obedient to the law of spiritual growth. Such a person will move continually forward — perhaps through deserts — but will advance toward this unknown country and will one day reach it, recapitulating in his or her own life the journey of God's chosen people.

John the Baptist[2]

The vocation of John the Baptist is intimately tied to the coming of the Word, to his Advent. It consists entirely of predicting, preceding, and preparing for his coming. And if the coming of the Word continues throughout the time of the church, if Jesus is always the one "who is coming," then we see that this vocation continues into every age.

God first calls upon John the Baptist to announce his coming. He will be called the "prophet of the Most High" (Luke 1:76). He takes his place among the series of prophets before him who had been called by God; and in one respect, his message is no different from theirs. Nevertheless, John the Baptist is unique among the prophets. He is "more than a prophet," as Jesus says of him (Luke 7:26). Indeed, he is not only a prophet, but in addition, he already participates in the eschatological events that the prophets had announced. These had prophesied that the coming of God would be prepared by "one who was sent." Isaiah had talked about "the voice of him who cries out in the desert: Prepare the way of the Lord" (40:3). In the book of Malachi, Yahweh says: "Behold, I am sending a messenger who will prepare the way before me" (3:1).

The difference between John the Baptist and the former prophets — and also his nearness to Jesus — appears as well in the contents of his prophecy. The substance of John's message is "to make salvation and the forgiveness of sins known to those who dwell in darkness and the shadow of death" (Luke 1:77, 79). Isaiah had also proclaimed that a light would one day shine on "those who walk in darkness and in the shadow of death" (9:1).

The Baptist's message is addressed to a world held captive by sin and death, powerless to free itself, a world destined for death and incapable of justice, a world without hope. And his happy vocation is to proclaim that all the bonds will be broken and that love will overcome. This is already the message of grace.

2. J. Daniélou, *Jean-Baptiste, témoin de l'Agneau* (Paris: Ed. du Seuil, 1964).

But it is not enough to say simply that John proclaims the imminence of grace; for with John, grace has already been unveiled. In this sense, John is the *precursor,* the one who walks ahead, but who is already part of the retinue: "He will go before him in the spirit and the power of Elijah" (Luke 1:17).

Taking Luke's Gospel, we see that the events surrounding the birth of John the Baptist are already an image of those surrounding Jesus' birth. The parallels are astonishing. Just as Jesus' birth will be announced to Mary, so John's birth had been announced to Zechariah, and in the same terms. Even more remarkable are the parallels between the births themselves. Advent thus appears as a pedagogy of the faith. Faith does not consist in the belief that God exists, but that God intervenes in history. This is what seems unreasonable to humans: that at the heart of the framework of ordinary events, in the midst of the determinism of physics and of the chains of sociological facts, there are irruptions of God — a properly divine activity — in which God creates, visits, and saves. This is what people cannot admit. It is true that we cannot offer any reason to justify this belief, but it is nevertheless through this that the living God reveals himself to us — the God who is coming, who enters into a personal relationship with us, and who forcefully rejects the abstract God of the deists, known by reason alone.

Joy is already given with John — not human joy, but messianic joy, that which Simeon called "the consolation of Israel." The angel says to Zechariah, "there will be joy and gladness for you, and many will rejoice in his name" (Luke 1:14). The joy that he will give already fills his own heart.

John's joy is not a secondary consequence. It is the very substance of his being. He is moved by divine joy, he bears witness to this joy, he is hidden in this joy; because the One who is coming, for whom John prepares, will give to his people the joy that the world cannot give, a joy beyond mere emotion. Just as John the Baptist prepares hearts for the heroic act of faith, he also prepares them for the joy that is almost too much to bear; he teaches the hearts accustomed to despair to open themselves to the happiness God has given. It is therefore not coincidental that the prayer of his feast day is a petition for spiritual joy.

John's message will nevertheless be a message of conversion: "He will go before him in the spirit and power of Elijah to turn the hearts of fathers toward children and the disobedient to the understanding of the righteous" (Luke 1:17). Because people are turned away from God, Adam's ancient sin continues to thrive in them. Now Adam's sin was the claim of being self-sufficient: "We have no need of God." Humankind claimed to assume its own destiny and to gain its own salvation; but through this, it destroyed itself, if it is true that humans exist and act only by virtue of dependence on the divine source. God thus enters into this world of sin.

John the Baptist is powerless to save this world. Even he, the greatest of the prophets, is aware that in this respect any amount of preaching is vain. He does not bring a new way of wisdom; he proclaims an event: this world of sin is going to be saved.

But he must still welcome this salvation. John does not ask sinners not to be sinners, because they were "conceived in sin." Instead, John asks them to recognize that they are sinners, to hate their sin, and to thirst for freedom from sin. This is the first conversion, which opens the heart and disposes it to grace. Of course, this conversion is already a grace. In this sense, John the Baptist is an instrument of grace. Now, people's hearts are hard. They are bound up in their lust and hatred. They are accustomed to their misery and cannot imagine that there could be something else. John the Baptist must therefore shake these hardened hearts. This is the tragic character of his mission. He himself is turned entirely toward the one who is to come. But he must lift the immense burden of the world's indifference surrounding him.

The one who bears witness to the light grapples with the darkness. The Gospel of John is constructed entirely upon this theme, and it begins with the Baptist. The one who bears witness to the light is intolerable to those who dwell in darkness, because he has come to disturb them. They are quite comfortable in this world of sin and do not like it when people bother them. John appears terrible to them: terrible because he speaks in the name of the demands of love; terrible because he does not participate in the illusion that has closed upon the world and that the Prince of this world keeps shut like a magic prison.

But John knows that he has the right to arouse hope, because he knows that hope will not be deceived. This is what gives him that extraordinary confidence. He has the right to proclaim salvation. "If Christ had not risen from the dead," St. Paul says, "we would be impostors." John is confident that the hope he has aroused will not be deceived.

III. The Different Times of Advent

The time of waiting includes a succession of moments. We have just seen how the Old Testament was the time of the first Advent. Then comes Christ, who is the total realization of everything that had been promised: in him our waiting is fulfilled, and God's plan is substantially accomplished. In Christ, God has given humankind everything he was able to give; creation finds its completion in him. God is perfectly glorified, and humanity is given the fullness of life, so that there will never be anything beyond Jesus Christ.

With Jesus Christ, the second Advent begins, which is no longer a waiting for God's gesture toward creation, but a waiting for the resounding of Christ's coming in the fullness of his Body. Christ's coming is comprised of two moments: first the Head, and then the Body. This mission makes up sacred history in the present time. It is the time during which everything that was acquired in Christ must penetrate into all things, communicating itself to everything that exists. This is the Advent in which we ourselves live, the waiting for the fullness of the Body of Christ, when "Christ will be all in all."

The cosmos itself will never be liberated until the liberation of human beings is fully realized through God's grace, beyond the frontiers of life and death. This is the cosmic vision of Christianity.

On this point, Fr. Teilhard de Chardin's project may help us to sufficiently widen the horizons of our vision so that we keep from becoming too narrow in our spirituality. A Christianity that would remain above all a private affair would be powerless to confront the modern world; it would leave Christians with a perpetual bad conscience next to those who are concerned with the solidarity of all humankind. On the contrary, it is to the extent that we give our Christianity this comprehensive dimension that it is able to respond to the call of today's world.

The very same Word of God through whom the stars exist, through whom the limits of the cosmos are established, has come to take hold of all things through his incarnation in order to bring them to completion. The Word of God will reclaim Adam and return him to the Father. In the Word, the relationship between God and humankind will reign supreme, first in the human nature of Jesus Christ, which is related entirely to him; then in every person, each of whom will have a part in the salvation brought in Jesus Christ.

These are the foundational certainties of the faith, upon which our lives' values establish themselves and gradually build themselves up.

CHAPTER TWO

Hope

Hope is the concrete expression of the Christian's attitude toward time. Hope, the "little green-eyed girl," is a great theological virtue and, as Péguy says, "the most difficult to practice. [. . .] We can still have a little faith, for you are so resplendent in your creation; a little charity, a little sympathy for our brothers; but hope is what's most difficult." Indeed, it is difficult to remain confident about the future when we are in the midst of difficulties. Our age is filled with despairing and discouraged people: this is, in fact, what characterizes the world in which we live.

Before speaking about hope in the biblical sense of the word, we will situate it, in its human context, with respect to two other attitudes that are totally different. A natural and spontaneous optimism, which is a human quality, is nothing but an inclination of the temperament: we find in people both optimistic temperaments and darker natures. There is nothing significant in this, except perhaps that it is more pleasant to live with people who see things through rose-colored glasses than with those whose glasses are somber. Hope is something completely different. A person who is generally pessimistic may also be filled with hope, which would be all the more beautiful; conversely, there may be people who are naturally optimistic, but who may never have a true hope and will therefore be inconstant. Hope in this sense defines itself in opposition to a certain kind of optimism and according to a certain kind of pessimism.

The Christian awaits something from time, from the coming events. This attitude contrasts with the stoic attitude, which consists in shielding oneself from events, saying "what is important is to discipline oneself and expect nothing." This stoic wisdom is seductive because it has the air of nobility and disinterestedness. Christians themselves are often accused of not being disinterested because they believe in happiness and because they work, in a sense, to achieve it. In reality, this accusation is something we must accept.

Stoicism is a way of fighting against suffering. Buddhists make the same argument: one must escape suffering; desire is the source of suffering; therefore, the best way to avoid suffering is to suppress all desire in oneself. As Gide said to Claudel, "I wish to die in perfect despair" (that is, having totally renounced the world of hope in an absolute serenity). We find this same attitude in much of contemporary thinking: "We should expect nothing, and simply do our best to exist."

Contrary to this apparent wisdom, the Christian believes in happiness and in the future. Christianity, after all, is not wisdom; it is faith.

Having situated the Christian attitude with respect to these other attitudes, which may seem seductive, we must learn how to reject them deliberately; we must know why we expect, believe in, and hope for something.

I. The Foundation of Hope

What gives us the right to hope? Why must we bear witness to hope? Hope is a virtue, something we experience, something difficult; it is a victory. We do not hope because things are going well; we hope when things are not going well. In other words, hope is based on something beyond immediate appearances.

Hope is based on God's promises, on the word of God: "I hope with a firm confidence that you will give me your grace in this world and eternal life in the next because you have promised me this."

Hope is hope in a person. We do not know much of what we hope for (What do we know of heaven? Very little), but we know in whom we hope. Having confidence in Christ, finding support in his words and in God's promises, is something unique to Christianity. This is very important, though it is often foreign to our aspirations. We could almost say that for many people today, one of the difficulties of hope is its superabundance. The beauty of Christianity is sometimes an obstacle to its credibility, whether because eternal participation in the beatitude of God seems excessive, or because people say, "That's more than we ask for; what we want is simply the satisfaction of our natural desires."

The idea of hope is pervasive in the Old Testament: "Yahweh is my rock, in whom I rest and find support. His promises shall never disappoint us." The attitude of hope is difficult for modern people because hope essentially consists in trusting someone. In people today, however, there is a well of defiance and mistrust. Because our trust has often been deceived, many of us have trouble ever trusting again.

Christian hope is particularly difficult because of the fact that it is only partially fulfilled, because for many people the effects of Christ's coming are not really apparent. They remain very much hidden. Many say: "If Christ were what you say he is, the whole face of the earth would have been changed. Well, it isn't; everything goes on just like it did before." Peter's second letter makes reference to this attitude: "Know that in the end times, scoffers will come, full of derision, saying, 'Where is the promise of his coming? From the time that our ancestors died, everything has remained as it was from the beginning of creation'" (2 Pet. 3:3-4).

On the other hand, Christ announced that he would return, and yet we have waited two thousand years for it. An active Christian faith may at times become tired of being ordered toward Christ's return. A doubt may creep up about what was promised, making trust difficult.

For a deeper reason, and one that is more significant for the spiritual life, trust is difficult because it requires a certain relinquishing of the self. To trust means to rely on another. However, we have learned to count on no one but ourselves. It is very hard for us to count on other people; we even have a tendency to make an ideal out of self-sufficiency and the ability to get through things on our own. We find dependence on others repugnant. We would prefer to keep control over things ourselves.

This attitude is already suspect on the human level because in the order of our human relationships we all, in fact, have need of each other and must be able to trust each other. This ability to lean on one another is precisely a form of love. The joyful recognition of our need for other people is not an expression of weakness, but the expression of our journey together toward God. Moreover, it is always reciprocal: if other people provide things for us, we provide things for other people. And even when we are plagued with self-doubt, even when we think we are useless, we have no idea to what extent other people find support in us on a mysterious level. The knowledge that other people are counting on us ought to be an idea that sustains us when we are ready to give up. The knowledge that other people need us is one of the things that bonds us more securely to life. Having others depend on us is fertile and beneficial on the human level, while the greatest suffering is to be of no use to anyone.

In the same way, our leaning on God, our counting on him, and our awaiting all things from him is not a lessening of ourselves. It is not a substitute for our own activity and initiative, as if it were a sort of *deus ex machina*. Rather, our dependence on God is a more profound penetration into the order of things, realizing they will ultimately be fulfilled by God alone, especially in the spiritual realm. This, moreover, is the proper character of hope: it allows us to strive for things that are beyond our power and that are possible for us only with God's help. In reality, the Christian life and the whole of Christianity is beyond our power: we are able to practice the gospel spirit and charity only because of the support God gives us. Only through God do we know what we strive for, and only by counting on him can we attain it. This attitude of leaning on God, of abandon, of rest in him is an essential aspect, the foundation of all other aspects, of hope. Hope is based on God's promise.

We must therefore discern in ourselves the manner in which we accept this attitude of trust in others and ultimately in God, not as a consequence of our own weakness, but as the very expression of the relationships that are constitutive of our existence. The whole Bible affirms that we can find support only in God, that we can await our salvation and the health of our souls only from God. In this is not a form of resignation; on the contrary, it is the expression of our relationship with God.

II. Hope Assumes the Orientation of Our Being toward Its Spiritual Fulfillment

The base of hope is a certain confidence in life, a certain taste for life and happiness. It is this natural confidence, this hope in the value of existence, which the grace of God perfects in us, but which, to a certain extent, it presupposes.

There may be people who are so beaten by life that this natural foundation is extinguished, people who are incapable of hope because their life seems so much a failure, and so they expect nothing. These people must first be healed on the natural level in order for grace to come and blossom within them. We must reawaken confidence in such people, whom we find all over the world, in whom there is a well of discouragement and, in extreme cases, despair. Love alone can save them: it is to the extent that one is loved, that is, to the extent that someone has confidence in one, that one is able to have confidence in oneself.

One of the best ways of loving is to expect something from another, because charity does not consist only in giving; it also consists in asking for something, in showing others that they can be useful. The greatest suffering for many people is to feel that their life has no value. This ends in a desperate feeling of solitude, of being cut off from the community.

We must be careful not to stifle other people. There is a way of being good that impedes others from being good. There are many forms of paternalism that often crush the people in its service. We must always be aware of the smallest gestures of goodwill, encourage them, and give them support. This is the true way of loving and helping others who are discouraged to believe in themselves again, to renew this confidence in themselves that will give them once again a desire for existence, for happiness, and for life. This is a profoundly Christian attitude because God is life, and the world he has created is good. To attach oneself to life, to believe in it, is to be profoundly in accordance with God's heart and with the meaning of creation. Not only does hope make us strive for our natural fulfillment, but it also adapts us and opens us to the spiritual completion of our being. This is what we say when we make the act of hope: "I hope for your grace in this world and for eternal life in the next."

But in practice, does the hope that many people have go beyond the level of human and worldly fulfillment? Is not supernatural hope beyond the horizon of many people? One of the things that seems most difficult to us today is to open our minds and hearts to total fulfillment, one that lies beyond the worldly point of view.

To this we must first respond that Christ's promise includes human fulfillment: he wishes to bring the whole of creation to fulfillment and completion. He has come to take hold of all that aspires to live, to understand, and to love, in order to bring it to its end. Everything that is valuable and good thus has a meaning. This fundamental Christian optimism, difficult to the extent that it is thwarted by sin, this aspiration for the success of God's work, this desire to make of our lives a collaboration with this work — such is the very foundation of what we call charity. Charity is not a matter of the emotions; it is the fact of having a life formed with, and by, God. Anything that forms itself in God will inevitably succeed, and anything that seems to impede or obstruct this success will eventually pass. To the extent that our lives are inserted into the accomplishment of God's work, they attain the absolute and become vocations.

On the other hand, anything in us that is a destructive force (like a tendency to disparage others in order to glorify ourselves), anything that ends in making others doubt themselves, anything in us that is mistrustful, anything that is a spirit of destruction, is fundamentally in opposition to Christ, and we ought to detest it: this is the spirit of the world. Destruction leads to more destruction, hostility leads to more hostility. Christ is never present in this, because Christ loves all that is, all that lives; he is the one who "will not quench the smoldering wick" (Matt. 12:20), who goes in search of the smallest act of goodwill in the most lost soul in order to try to bring it back to life. In the midst of all that is mediocre in us, he finds the love that still subsists in order to try patiently to make it grow. He acts always in the direction of the positive realization of God's work.

Hope, in this sense, has nothing individualistic or selfish about it, because it brings us to desire the accomplishment of God's work in others as well as ourselves. Now it is sometimes easier to hope for others than it is for ourselves. There are people who believe in heaven but who have trouble accepting that they could ever reach it because of all that they feel is unfinished and resistant in themselves. The disinterested conception of hope goes beyond *me* and *you* by desiring that God's work be accomplished in me as well as in anyone else. Thus we have the obligation to desire our own salvation and to love ourselves. We may commit a serious sin of a lack of self-love when we do violence to ourselves. One of the saddest things to see is the lives that have sunk down into wine, drugs, or eroticism. We must view this with an unreserved clarity: by passing from degradation to degradation, infidelity to infidelity, many people reach the point of shutting themselves up completely from God, becoming fixed in attitudes of ambition or materialism, and ending with a feeling of failure and total disgust with themselves.

We thus have the obligation to accomplish the masterpiece the Holy Spirit wishes to make of us: "Do not grieve the Holy Spirit," St. Paul tells us (Eph. 4:30). We have the absolute obligation to collaborate with him and to be obedient to him. The Spirit edifies, forms, and instructs us. Hope consists in always remaining open to the Holy Spirit and to strive for the spiritual fulfillment of our lives and every life.

Ultimately, the entire world has no other object than to give rise to the communion and growth of God's children. It is, as Bergson says, "the melting pot in which gods are made," and what matters is not the unfurling of the vicissitudes of history, but rather whatever of the eternal is built up through this apparent framework of history. In our age many people take history for the whole of reality. However, when we compare the brevity of the time in our life that belongs to history and the eternity of the life of God it so quickly emerges into, when we consider the immense universe of the living who live the life of God, the surface of history appears to be, as our fathers said in the past, a time of trials.

This time of trials is given to us so that we can make manifest our choice for Love. It is an extremely short time, but one in which eternity is decided. That is why St. Catherine of Siena said: "Let us not wait for the time that does not wait for us; let us give our lives to our brothers." Most people reach the hour of death without ever having committed serious crimes, but with the horrible regret of having just missed Love. They feel that they could have filled their lives with love when, instead, they had been nothing but mediocre. In God's light, then, they will judge themselves unmercifully, because, in fact, we are not judged, but we judge ourselves. That is why we have the right and the obligation to dedicate ourselves more and more to the service of Love, like so many lights and graces of God, to order our lives toward Christ's work, and to make this understood by others. We are obliged to give people this warning, because it would be unjust to allow people to remain ignorant of what could give greatness and value to their lives.

This is how some critics have interpreted Pascal's Wager. For Pascal, they say, the Wager does not consist so much in choosing between the whole of life and eternity, but it consists in saying to the free-thinkers: "Just make an eight-day retreat during which you think only of God and you deprive yourself of your normal satisfactions. What do you have to lose? Only eight days of free-thinking. If nothing happens, you can go back to it afterward; consequently, your stakes are small, and you have the chance of winning eternity." Pascal believes that there would be something decisive in this, because if a person truly made a retreat, he could not help but encounter God in some way, and that could not help but amount to a positive gain. There is no doubt that most people never make a retreat and never take this time to reflect seriously on the meaning of their lives. They are constantly swept about by circumstances without ever having reflected on what might be able to give their lives a certain weight. The only thing that can give weight to a life is Love.

The essence of hope frees itself from all of this: it is a striving towards the spiritual fulfillment of life, the obligation to bring about the accomplishment of God's work. It consists first in the fact of having entrusted ourselves to God, next in the obligation to bring about what is best in ourselves and in others, and to believe that this is possible, even though it takes time, perhaps all of eternity. For life is ultimately a process of deification, a gradual transformation of every human soul by the Spirit. We must come to understand that we are taken up into this movement and try to live in accordance with it, to realize that each of us is united to all others, who are themselves taken up, and that we are striving toward a particular goal. In this our lives are enlightened and find their meaning.

III. Hope Means Patience

Patience is the aspect of hope emphasized most in the Old and New Testaments. "Therefore, since we have been justified by faith," writes St. Paul, "we have peace with God through our Lord Jesus Christ, through whom we have gained access by faith to this grace in which we stand firm, and we boast in hope of the glory of God. Not only that, we even boast of our tribulations, knowing that tribulations produce endurance, a proven character of endurance, and a proven character of hope. And hope does not deceive because the love of God has been poured into our hearts by the Holy Spirit that has been given to us" (Rom. 5:1-5).

For St. Paul, authentic hope is thus a hope that has confronted difficulties and obstacles. Hope is a virtue, something potent, a certain ability to hold fast and endure despite all sorts of obstacles, to undergo failure like a pebble on the seashore when the waves beat upon it and break against it. To be sure, our hopes are shaken by failures, contradictions, and disappointments. We must therefore pass from human hope to spiritual hope. In other words, we must not make our love for God dependent on what he may or may not give us, according to what we would like. To become angry with God when God tests us is only human. But we must not lose our faith because we have undergone failures, no matter what sort of failures they may be. Hope is a certain capacity to maintain our expectation for happiness and our faith in it despite our trials.

This hope must survive even through spiritual trials, which are more difficult. It is hard for us to continue to hope when, having made a thousand resolutions, we have continually been unable to keep them; or when, having exerted the best of our efforts, we find that we are at the same point as before and have not made any progress; or when we experience the extent of our difficulties in attaining spiritual growth. Hope is then something very brave, but even more, it becomes something beautiful and noble. And we will be judged more for our theological virtues than we will for our moral virtues.

To put it another way, the practice of the moral virtues depends largely on our temperaments. In spite of their imperfections, there may be people who have a great quality of love for God, while people who seem to be perfect may have little real love for God. The theological virtues make use of the materials they find in people. It is possible that sinners, throughout a life of sin, may keep from "letting go" of God, and may fight their entire lives in order finally to reach love. Their lives are more valuable in God's eyes than those that seem more ordered, but in which this intensity of love is missing. What is essential is that, through the various trials that life may present to us, hope strengthens itself into a confidence in God, in his forgiveness, in his help, and in the accomplishment of his plan, which then endures the test of time.

Patience is the ability to stand fast in time; for time erodes — or, at least, it erodes certain things. Time wears away anything that is the concern of superficial people, but it does not wear away — in fact, it increases — that which is the concern of spiritual people. This is the difference between routine and fidelity. Going to Mass might at certain times become simply a sort of habit, but it could also be a matter of fidelity, that is, perseverance, even during the times of an interior emptiness and dryness. This continuity in time is the very condition for passing from the surfaces to the depths of love. Our love for God is not profound unless it has thus passed the test of time, because it will have in this way rooted itself in the depths of our being, in something essential that is not related to our moods or feelings. The saints and mystics call these moments "nights," when love has no resonance in our feelings or in our imagination and when the things that have to do with God take on a character of deprivation for us.

Whether it is a matter of nights in the love of God or nights in the love of others (because there are times when our love for others has this character, when for no other reason but fidelity, even though it greatly annoys us, we nevertheless do something for someone else or participate in such and such an activity), all spiritual authors say that it is to the extent that we will have been able to endure these "nocturnal" periods that we will then be able to rediscover things with a renewed depth. Through the test of time, the interior person — that is, the real person — strengthens him- or herself.

At the beginning of our spiritual lives, we are unformed, and so we must gradually become formed. We are made up only of possibilities, and we must gradually actualize these. We cannot do this prematurely, but we can make gradual advances, that is, we can find the essential axes of our being and then enter into our decisions with freedom, progressively drawing from the depths of our soul the face Christ loves and which will one day blossom in his light.

This is not simply a private affair, but by espousing God's total gesture throughout the whole of history, this hope has a predominantly missionary spirit, because it has the power of a desire that affects even those that are distant. Hope has a creative character that mysteriously affects the distant depths of humankind. It has the efficacy of a missionary prayer that obeys unknown laws. And Christ has said that this missionary prayer has always been granted.

The bold prayers of the saints effect the salvation of the world in the same way that Christ saved the world: not by his external acts, but by the infinite nature of his love. Along with St. Catherine of Siena, we believe in the infinite nature of desire, in the mysterious action of love that goes beyond external gestures (gestures that vary according to the diversity of vocations), fundamentally to fulfill the striving toward the full realization of the kingdom of God.

CHAPTER THREE

Missionary Hope in the Old Testament

We ask the Lord to awaken a hope in our souls that will bear us above all those things that sometimes threaten to paralyze us in the immediate, so that we may fix our eyes on God's promise. A hope that animates our interior life and allows us to help others to hope is one of the roles the Christian must take in a despairing world, a world that often resigns itself to its circumstances. If our hope is alive, it will communicate itself.

I. The Theme of the New Jerusalem

Isaiah 60, a vast song of hope, is one of the greatest examples of this expectant waiting in the Old Testament. It is centered around the theme of the New Jerusalem, which will later fill the book of Revelation. The close of Revelation will describe the New Jerusalem as the fulfillment of all hope. Here in Isaiah 60, the earthly Jerusalem is the image of the definitive city of God toward which all things tend.

One of the present pastoral and catechetical difficulties is that people today are mostly "city dwellers" who have little sympathy with the symbols borrowed from rural life: oil, wine, bread, etc. But we must not forget that the Bible also contains a network of symbols from the city which, moreover, was not easy to develop.

At the start of David's reign, the city was something to be cursed. Babel was the symbol of Satan's city, and it seemed as if only the nomads in the desert in their lives of shepherding were able to encounter God. With David, there is something of a reversal of history: Jerusalem becomes the Holy City, and thus the idea that a city could be something holy appears. We find in the Old Testament at once a repugnance for the city, which seems to be associated with the world of sin, and a sort of sanctification of the city, which has become the symbol of the city of God.

Our contemplation must penetrate the realities of our age; it cannot be tied simply to the past. To contemplate means to discover the divine content of the world in which we are living. It is a matter of perspective; that is, the same thing may signify two different realities. For example, the crowd of people in the metro may seem to us to be a foreign world; but if we take into our perspective the fact that God is present there and that he loves each of the souls that make up this crowd, our trip can become a wonderful prayer. It is sometimes easier to pray in the midst of others than isolated from them, because their presence can be a source of prayer if our perspective allows us to discover the divine meaning of all things.

This is very important for laypeople, whose vocation is to discover God, not outside of the world (as monks do), but within the world. If it were only possible to discover God by separating ourselves from the world, the life of the layperson would be a contradiction in terms. It is not outside of life that we must discover God, but within our lives; for in reality, this is where he is hidden. Praying means coming to recognize God in all the realities that fill our daily lives and consequently making these realities a means of going to him, because they come from him and he speaks to us through them. Everything that first appears to be an obstacle becomes a means. Through it we rediscover paradise and we live in God's presence.

For the heart filled with God, everything speaks of him, and everything, in a certain way, comes down to him. This is something we can experience: a teacher, evaluating his students' compositions, aware of the children's souls that are before him, is able to make a wonderful prayer if he sees them in relation to God. It is an error to believe that we cannot integrate prayer with life.

It is wonderful to see that the Bible presents the city to us as a symbol of the city in which all of God's children are gathered with God dwelling in their midst. Let us thus avoid placing the New Jerusalem outside of our present life, but rather try to see it as the projection of which our earthly cities are only imperfect sketches. In other words, everything that people today strive to construct through their vast cities is ultimately an image of the city of God. The assembled masses, the human unity fashioned together: this is everything Isaiah is talking about. But these efforts on the part of humankind are only an imperfect sketch that our vision and our hearts must extend by desire. And this vision is more than just a symbol: there is a deeper continuity between the earthly and heavenly city. We are working for something that will ultimately end in the heavenly Jerusalem, where all human efforts — and not only the reality of the cosmos — will be in some way transfigured.

Berdiaev says that the cathedrals are like images that we will no longer need in heaven, because there we will possess the reality itself. We still live in a world of signs and symbols; but through these signs and symbols, we tend toward the realities that are the completions of God's plan. Hope means entering into a contemplation of the eternal city toward which all humankind tends. This is what the beautiful passage in the Letter to the Romans says: "The whole of creation hopes that it will be set free from slavery and corruption in order to share in the glorious freedom of the children of God. The whole of creation is groaning in labor pains" (8:20-22).

If we were to experience more deeply the fact that the city of God is coming to birth in the midst of humanity's trials on earth, if we were to see the progress and the crises of the world from the perspective of Christian hope as the labor pains for the birth of some-

thing destined to live on eternally, our engagement with these realities would take on its full spiritual significance, and our activity
would be pervaded with the spirit of prayer and the light of hope.

II. A Commentary on Isaiah 60

Here we will explore three principal themes: the veil that is torn
asunder, the gathering, and the thirst for the resurrection.

"Yahweh rises up, and his glory shines upon you as the darkness
covers the earth" (Isa. 60:1-2). The first goal of hope is that the veil
be torn asunder so that we can see God. "You made us for Yourself,
Lord, and our hearts are restless until they rest in You," as St.
Augustine said. We were made in order to contemplate God, in
order to see him. Only the contemplation of the Blessed Trinity will
fill our hearts and beatify our intelligence.

In effect, God is hidden from many people. He seems absent to
them, and they manage without him. We would have to suffer from
this impenetrability but for our profound hope to see the darkness
subside so that we can contemplate God face to face. This hope is
expressed in the beautiful lines from the *Adoro Te:*

Jesu quem velatum nunc aspicio
Oro fiat illud quod tam sitio
Ut te revelata cernens facie . . .[3]

There is a very beautiful tension between *velatum* and *revelata:*
"For the moment, You are still veiled. I am able to grasp You only
through veils. Faith alone allows me to reach You in a crust of bread,
and I desire for these veils to be drawn back."

To reveal means, in the proper sense of the word, "to unveil."

---

3. Jesus, now veiled before me,
   I pray for that for which I thirst so much:
   To see you unveiled.

Occasionally the veil is torn a bit, a small ray of light passes through it and touches us, and for a moment we experience what divine joy may be like. But these are only transient graces that keep alive our fundamental orientation toward the vision of God. Certainly nothing else is capable of satisfying our intelligence and our hearts so much as this vision of God that Christ has promised us.

This is the world that the prophet Isaiah heralds in the New Jerusalem: "God's glory will manifest itself" (60:2). "Then you shall be radiant at what you see, your heart shall throb and overflow" (60:5).

After our long time of waiting, after our long separation, when the vision of God overflows and excites our hearts and causes them to throb, we will live by that divine joy that beatifies, and that reaches into the depths of our being. We are as yet only half alive, and we will only be fully alive once we are submerged in the life of God overflowing within us.

It is then that our intelligence, which has been created neither for erudition, nor for dilettantism, nor for inventing technical means, but rather for contemplating the Being of things, will behold God himself. Only those who understand what the intelligence is made for can be called intelligent. They are unfortunate who would distrust the intelligence — it is such a noble gift from God — but also those who would fail to understand that the intelligence itself is engaged in the drama of existence, that there are sins of the intelligence, and that these sins are more serious because they affect humankind in what is most essential.

The sanctity of the intelligence is found in being ordered toward the grasping of truth in its fullness. But our world is filled with wounded intelligences. It is one of the aspects of original sin that we perhaps too often neglect because, through a false understanding of sincerity, we confuse intelligence with intellectual ability. What in fact makes up the intelligence is a knowledge of truth. There are certain people who are proud of their intellectual abilities, and who nevertheless have wounded, sick, and destructive intelligences (destructive because a distorted intelligence distorts those around it).

This drama of error is one of the most tragic aspects of the world of sin.

Hope, on the contrary, is a profound dynamism of the spirit which thirsts for the fullness of light, which fixes its eyes upon this light in the darkness, which strives to emerge from the darkness in order to be bathed in the light of the Trinity, to be illuminated and transfigured by it. Life is given to us so that we may enter into truth. This is why knowledge of Christ is so important: it is to the extent that we love Christ that we are able to live through him. St. Augustine expresses well the idea that the intelligence is made for the contemplation of God when he says: "Our soul is restless until it rests in You"; *Tu es, Deus, Amor meus* ("You, O God, are my love").

We must begin by freeing ourselves from the chains that paralyze us; next we must continue always to strive, through the inner movements of desire, toward the light that will not be possessed in its fullness until the very end. In this is a fundamental Christian attitude: an *élan,* a sort of weight draws us through all things toward God and allows us to discover him in everything.

The central theme of Isaiah 60 is that of "gathering": "The nations walk by your light. Look around you and see: they all gather and come toward you. Your sons come from afar and your daughters are carried on their arms" (60:3-4). "What are these that fly along like clouds, like doves to their cotes?" (60:8). The image is very beautiful: the dove-cote is the New Jerusalem. "All the ships are gathering for me, with the ships of Tarshish in the lead" (60:9). (Tarshish undoubtedly refers to Spain and the Moors arriving from across the Mediterranean.)

The Gathering of Israel

The dispersion of Israel was a reality before the time of waiting for the Messiah. The Jews had been scattered in the Exile, and Isaiah expresses the desire of God's people for a gathering together and reunification. But through this temporal dimension, the gathering of the visible Israel, there already appears the desire for the gathering of the whole Israel, the new people of God that will encompass all of God's children.

This is an expression of the whole of human hope: humankind is made for God and cannot find beatitude except in union with him. Secondly, humanity is made to live in community. We are not made to live alone, but to develop ourselves in an exchange with others. It is essential to us to be in communication and in communion. In this is the mystery of personal life, which makes of the exchange between persons an essential aspect of existence. This is first realized in the first pages of the Bible, in the union of man and woman: "It is not good for man to be alone" (Gen. 2:18).

The creation of Eve is the first expression of this community, which finds its fulfillment in children. It is equally true of other forms of communion between people, and with Christ: this aspiration emerges into an intense spiritual communion that is called the body of Christ, whose many members are all in solidarity with each other.

Having said that we suffer from impenetrability, we may also add here that we suffer from division. The impossibility of communion wounds something so deep in us that we end by falling into despair. The number of people who despair of being able to communicate, who feel closed up within an incurable solitude, is immense. Hope requires that we surmount this despair, in the same way that it requires us to surmount the apparent impenetrability.

The impossibility of a total communion, by virtue of impenetrability and of people's constant refusal to be open to each other, seems evidence of the difficulty of making people live together in peace and of the ceaseless recurrence of conflicts. Hope in the Word of God, however, allows us to believe in the possibility of total communion, of perfect harmony, and of openness between people, at the level of a people who would gather together all humanity. This love for others, which is borne in us as a thirst, and whose fulfillment is so difficult, will be wholly fulfilled in the New Jerusalem, which will assemble all of God's people.

The Assembly of God's People

The New Jerusalem — this is an essential point of the text — will gather together not only God's people but also all of those who were outside. This text is an eminently missionary one. It is one of the rare texts in the Old Testament that speaks of the conversion of nations: "the nations, the wealth of nations shall come to you: the nations walk toward your light" (60:3). "The sons of foreign lands shall rebuild your walls" (60:10). And note also this image, which is so beautiful: "Your gates shall always be open; day and night, they shall not be closed but shall admit to you the wealth of nations, and their kings in the vanguard" (60:11).

This would have been an extraordinary idea for a Jew — so extraordinary that it was not understood. And this text, though it is relatively old, had little influence in the development of the history of Israel: the Jews in Christ's time had a much more rigid notion of the people of God.

We see a sort of bursting open in this text, a remarkable broadening. And we could say that this is one of the Old Testament texts in which divine inspiration is certain: the prophet's perspective reaches a level of vision that infinitely surpasses that of the people of his time. He bursts all boundaries. This is what prophetic vision does. It transcends all immediate realities; it penetrates deeply into the abyss of the future and shows the prior realization of something that, at first glance, had seemed impossible.

For us, this is an essential aspect of our prayer. And missionary hope invites us, despite apparent impossibilities, to believe that all of the peoples of Islam, of India, and of secularized countries are called to participate in the city of God; to believe that God's grace is sufficiently powerful to level all obstacles. This tells us to what extent the missionary attitude is hope — a heroic hope. It must prevail over all evidence to the contrary, because the great temptation is to settle into, and become content with, a situation as we find it. Thus when John XXIII announced that the goal of the council was ecumenism, he had received one of those prophetic inspirations that tumbles walls, that makes holes in seemingly permanently established obstacles. How many people thirty years ago would seriously have been able to imagine that there could be a true movement toward reconciliation among Protestants, Catholics, and Orthodox? The prophetic vision and triumphal hope do not come to a stop at apparent impossibility. They force the event, and by that very act they determine the possibility of what seemed unachievable.

What is true for the separation of Christians is also true for the nations of the world; and our prayer must already work ahead in hope for the gathering together of all peoples — first, in the visible Jerusalem, in the belief that all people are capable of recognizing Christ's salvation; and, moreover, in the invisible Jerusalem, in which all people of goodwill will one day assemble to make up the city of God.

The Thirst for the Resurrection

Following the humble thirst for God and the humble thirst for communion, the final aspect of hope is the humble thirst for the resurrection, that is, the desire to be freed from the slavery that is related to the body: sickness, the heaviness that holds us down, and the weight of death, which constitutes the very law of the life of our bodies. The triumphal hope of the Christian is a feeling that even this is a false appearance and can be overcome, because there is no obstacle that the power of divine grace will not one day conquer.

If we truly lived this in the very depths of our being, what a difference it would make in our attitude toward existence! There would first of all be a sort of fundamental dynamism, because we are moving unshakably toward the fulfillment of all things. On the other hand, as St. Paul says, the trials of this world would seem much smaller to us next to "the eternal weight of glory" (2 Cor. 4:17). We would better come to realize that we are in a time in which things are being formed, and that they will finally open into the beyond.

Hope must thus inspire us to confront obstacles: in the confrontation of the drama of faith that brings us to discover God; in the confrontation of the drama of love that brings us to desire communion with others in spite of the difficulties, and to work toward being agents of peace by continually creating love and communion; and, finally, in the battle against the weight of people's physical and material suffering, by trying to relieve it as much as possible. All of this is already an anticipation of the resurrection. This is what the text of Isaiah 60 tells us, in the last part that describes the new cosmos: "The sun shall no longer be your light by day, nor shall the moon's brightness shine upon you by night; Yahweh shall be your light forever, and your God shall be your glory" (60:19). This idea is taken up again in chapter 66, which is an extension of chapter 60: "As the new heavens and the new earth which I will make shall endure before me, so shall your race and your name endure. From one new moon to the next, and from one sabbath to the next, all flesh shall come to bow down before me" (66:22-23). These texts affirm the new world of the resurrection in which even our bodies will be brought to life by God's glory.

We allow the Holy Spirit to renew this immense hope within us, to renew our inner striving toward that which God's love has destined for us, so that the dynamism of our lives helps us to overcome the difficulties of the present, as we strive toward the light, trying to pull others along into the dynamism of divine hope.

PART THREE

The Mysteries of Christ the Redeemer

CHAPTER ONE

The Mystery of Christ and the Three Times of Advent

Prayer is an occasion to deepen our understanding of the inexhaustible riches of Christ *(investigabiles divitiae Christi)*, of which St. Paul speaks. The mystery of Christ by himself is an immense universe of which we still know practically nothing. We must therefore humbly ask the Blessed Virgin to help us enter a little more deeply into the mystery of her Son. Along with the human and secular sciences, the knowledge of Christ is the sum total of all wisdom and science; it is the only science capable of revealing to us the ultimate secret of all things.

We have already meditated upon the waiting for Christ in the Old Testament, the first time of Advent that prepares God's people for his coming. Christ is the fulfillment of this waiting. In him, as the beautiful text from the Second Letter to the Corinthians says, "the Amen" has been uttered, God's promise has been fulfilled, and all things have been accomplished (1:20). But what has been accomplished in Christ must be extended into the whole of humankind. We are still in a time of waiting: there is a second time of Advent, which is a waiting for the coming of the Word in the Church, his interior and missionary coming. Finally, there will be a third time of Advent, the waiting for the return of Christ in his glory when he will definitively establish his kingdom.

St. Bernard has often discussed the theme of the three times of Advent, the three Parousias, the three Comings. All three are hailed in Psalm 117:26: *Benedictus qui venit.* In Greek, the meaning is reinforced by the use of the substantive: blessed is "the Coming." "He who comes" is one of the names of Christ. On Palm Sunday the children hailed the Messiah with this verse: "Hosanna to the Son of David," *benedictus qui venit* (Matt. 21:9). Our Lord tells us (Matt. 23:39) that he will be greeted on the day of the final Parousia with this same hymn, and it is with this hymn as well that we hail his coming in the Eucharist at every Mass. We are thus able to meditate upon these three times of Advent, trying to understand all of their riches and their different dimensions.

I. The First Advent:
The Waiting in the Old Testament Is Fulfilled in Christ

We are no longer in the Old Testament stage, because the waiting in the Old Testament has been fulfilled in Christ; the end of all things has been reached in him. In the present time, we await the unfolding of what has been accomplished in Christ. As Isaiah says, "Remember no longer the things of the past; behold, I shall perform new wonders. I shall make a path across the sea"; in other words, Christ recapitulates, accomplishes, and brings to fulfillment everything that had been begun in the Old Testament.

What is it that has been accomplished in Christ such that we are able to see in him the full realization of God's plan, and believe that the decisive event of history has occurred? In Christ, God is perfectly glorified; God's sanctity is perfectly loved and recognized. The end of all creation is this glory of God. All of the sacrifices of the Old Testament and even those of all peoples are ordered toward him. The act of offering a victim to God is the expression of human effort to acknowledge God's domain. People take something that belongs to them and set it apart for God: this is the meaning of all sacrifice. But this remains something imperfect, as the Letter to the Hebrews explains (9:11-15): God does not attach importance to the blood of goats and heifers, but rather to the gifts that come from the heart.

The only thing that has worth in God's eyes is a love freely given. The only sacrifice is our hearts' true homage to God. And St. Paul shows us the perfect sacrifice in the mystery of Christ on the cross, that is, in the event by which God is perfectly glorified. "For the Lamb in their midst shall be their shepherd and shall lead them to the springs of life, and God shall wipe every tear from their eyes" (Rev. 7:13-17). In his passion, Christ appeared as the true Lamb who perfectly fulfilled that which was, in the Old Testament, the mystery of the paschal lamb. John the Baptist had indicated Christ at the time of his baptism by the name "the Lamb of God." It is by this name as well that we proclaim his coming in the Eucharist: "Lamb of God who takes away the sins of the world." The mystery of the Lamb is no longer the infinite love of God, but the infinite and gratuitous love fulfilled in Christ.

In order to understand this better, we recall the episode of the paschal lamb in the Old Testament. At the time of the flight from Egypt, the angel of death destroyed every firstborn and spared the houses marked with the blood of the lamb. The lamb is thus sacrificed in the place of the firstborn of the Jews. This is the mystery of substitution: Christ has substituted himself in our place in order to bear the weight of divine anger and justice, that is, the weight of the incompatibility of sin and sanctity. This is one of the most mysterious and important aspects of Christ's passion. Though we are sinners, Christ has saved us by bearing the weight of our sin. By virtue of his intervention, like that of the lamb in the Old Testament, mercy triumphs: "By this we have come to know love: while we were sinners, Christ laid down his life for us" (1 John 3:16).

"All have sinned and are deprived of God's glory, and they are freely justified by his grace, by means of the redemption in Jesus Christ. God has surrendered him as expiation through faith, by his blood, in order to manifest his justice" (Rom. 3:23-26). Christ redeems a multitude of sins by setting in opposition to sin, which is the fact of man's having preferred himself to God, the perfect act of obedience by which, on the contrary, Christ manifests that God ought to be preferred above everything. Christ's passion is the expression of a love that makes him "obedient to death and to death on the Cross" (Phil. 2:8). St. Augustine has defined sin as the "love of self to the neglect of God" and opposes to this the "love of God to the neglect of self." Christ says, "My food is to do the will of my Father" (John 4:34), thus bearing witness to the overflowing sanctity of God's will.

In Christ's passion the end of creation is achieved, because God will never be loved more than he is by Christ — that is, by the human nature assumed by the Word — on the cross. Henceforward, we can offer to God only this infinite love by which Christ loved him, and this is the whole meaning of the sacrifice of the Mass. The height of the Mass is this offering to God, this perfect glorification: "Through Him, with Him, and in Him, all glory and honor are Yours, Almighty Father." Because it is the essential act of offering to God the infinite love by which Christ loved him, the Eucharist is the end and completion of all things. That is why we can center the whole of the history of the world around the phrase of the Mass in which Christ, the High Priest, returns all things to his Father. By this, Christ brings to completion the worship of the temple and every other sacrificial aspect of the Old Testament.

This attitude is at the heart of a missionary spirituality. We also must lay down our lives for our sisters and brothers. Just as Christ came to find us, who were lost, so we must continue this act and go ourselves to look for those who are lost. We have been loved not only in the sense of having been created, but also in the sense that we have been ransomed. We must not allow ourselves only to live in the paradise of those saved, as Christ living in the glory of his Father. But, as Christ left his Father's house, so, too, must we go out to those who have been abandoned, substituting ourselves for them, interceding for them, and, as the saints have done, wishing to bear ourselves the weight of suffering due to sin in order to deliver them and save them.

In this is the mysterious participation in the work of redemption that continues in the body of Christ. We continue to save the pagan world to the extent that we offer ourselves for it in the way that Christ offered himself for us: "I am fulfilling in my flesh what was lacking in Christ's passion" (Col. 1:24).

This attitude must precede every external act. And this is the admirable case in some sick people who offer the whole of their lives for the salvation of the pagans. Every form of life is able to be effective in this sense. This is the marvelous aspect of the communion of saints, which truly works for the salvation of the world through its charity.

"One of the soldiers thrust his lance into his side, and immediately blood and water flowed out" (John 19:34). John is the only one of the Evangelists who refers to this fact of Christ's passion. The Fathers of the Church have believed that therefore this fact is rich in meaning for John. The water and blood flowing from Christ's side is a symbol that Christ's passion is a source of life. Perhaps John had in mind that scene in the creation of humans in which Eve was taken from Adam's side? In any event, the Church Fathers have always seen in this aspect of Christ's passion the birth of the Church, the new Eve who comes from the pierced side of Christ. The blood of Christ here appears as the principle of new life. It is the sacrament of the life of the Spirit (this is the meaning of the liturgy for the Feast of the Precious Blood). It establishes a new and definitive creation: the creation of the authentic man, the authentic woman, Christ and the church.

"This is why," the author of the Letter to the Hebrews tells us, "not even the first covenant could be inaugurated without the shedding of blood. . . . Thus Christ, offered once to take away the sins of many, will appear a second time, without sin, in order to bring salvation to those who wait for it" (9:18-28). There are a number of themes in this epistle. I would like especially to make use of the idea of the blood of the covenant, which makes reference to the central event in Exodus in which Moses, having sacrificed a victim, poured its blood over the people and the altar in order to mark the relationship between God and his people. In the liturgy of the Eucharist, we say: "Behold, the blood of the New Covenant." The Eucharist is a new aspect of the decisive action accomplished by Christ. The sharing of the same blood is the efficacious sign of our communion with God and with our sisters and brothers. Although the sacramental signs sometimes remain external and confused for us, they ought to help us grasp how, in Christ, the whole time of Israel's waiting is fulfilled, and to deepen our understanding of the meaning of its mystery. In Christ the perfect covenant is accomplished, and there can be no union more perfect than the union of God and humanity in Christ.

"Are you the one who is to come, or must we wait for another?" asks St. John the Baptist (Matt. 11:3). And Our Lord responds to John's disciples, "Look and see these signs." We are not waiting for another. This is what distinguishes the Christian from those who look to the future to bring salvation, whatever it may be. As for us, we affirm that all waiting has been fulfilled. Yet there often remains in us a source of anxiety that causes us to look elsewhere, because we are not aware that we already possess everything we could desire, and even more. We must learn that Christ is sufficient for us. Prayer means to stop at, and enter into possession of, the treasures we have already been given. Christ is the expression of the perfect glory of God, of perfect love, and of the definitive creature that we must become.

II. The Second Advent and the Time of the Church

What was accomplished in Christ was accomplished only in order that it may be communicated to every person. Christ is at once he who has come and he who is to come. He is always the one who is to come. The risen Christ, in whom all people are already saved, communicates a life that strives to fill all things. Christ is the Head, but his Body is still being formed. And the time of the Church is the time of the unfolding of Christ. What was accomplished in him unfolds itself in two ways: in each of us, on one hand; and in the whole of humankind, on the other.

We must allow Christ to pervade our souls to the extent that he becomes all in all; we must, according to St. Paul's beautiful expression, "put on" Christ (Rom. 13:14), trying to be what he was, such that we truly become his disciples. The whole of the Christian life is this progressive evangelization of our being, this shedding of the flesh, selfish and closed up within ourselves, this opening up to Christ's teachings that we must follow. We must, like him, become poor; we must learn to love our sisters and brothers, and turn ourselves toward the Father. The saints have often spoken of this transformation of humankind in Jesus Christ. We are taken up into a process, namely that of the Holy Spirit working within us in order to accomplish a certain spiritual fulfillment in us. The Christian life consists in allowing the Holy Spirit to transform us gradually into Christ. The unique end of every person is to become another Christ, because only the one who is transformed into Christ may enter into the Father's house. This is not a matter of choice or of preference; it is the sole purpose of existence.

This is true of all people, even those who are far from Christ: every Muslim, every Marxist will one day have to be totally transformed into Christ in order to enter into the Father's house; for in the future city of God, there will no longer be any Muslims, atheists, Christians, or Jews. There will be only Jesus Christ, Head and Body, gathering all people together. This is the remarkable unification of our worldview.

A distant preparation is required for this formation of the body of Christ. Anyone who has an instinct for love and an instinct for charity knows well that we do not reach others by doing violence to them, but rather by sharing in what they are and by knowing how to bring them to take the first steps, which are merely preparatory, but which move towards a meaning that may one day lead them to Christ. Most of the time, it is not a matter of immediately announcing Christ to them, but of beginning initial preparations, which consist of removing distant obstacles, answering certain objections, and inspiring certain attitudes that direct these people along the lines of their search, such that they create the essential conditions for salvation. It makes no difference whether these preparations grow and expand, or even if they do not lead to Christ during the lifetime of those who initiated them.

The Church teaches that every soul that sincerely searches for God already possesses sanctifying grace. There are thus non-Catholics who already live by grace, without being aware of it, to the degree that they are open to it. We must learn how to bring about this first conversion, which is a conversion of people to better themselves, before being an authentic conversion to Christ. This initial conversion already brings them to live the life of Christ. Every person is immersed in the life of the Spirit. We could say that this life waits only for the very first fissures in the shell of egotism that threatens to trap people, in order to penetrate into their souls. The Spirit knocks constantly at the door of every heart. The Holy Spirit pervades the totality of humankind more than we would think. But the center of his action is the Church in the strict sense of the word; because it is to his Spouse, the Church, that the Word has given his Spirit.

On the one hand, "the Spirit of the Lord fills the world and is all-embracing" (Wis. 1:7), and no aspect of humanity is foreign to him. Not only must Christ be "all," he must also be "in all." The grace of Christ reaches every person from within, for no person is a stranger to the solicitations of grace. On the other hand, this grace is proclaimed and communicated through the Church so that all people may have access to the life of Christ by participating in the life of the sacraments. Through his perpetual coming to humankind and to each person in particular, Christ thus takes on his definitive structure, and his Body is formed in every nation.

This second coming of Christ to humankind makes the present a time of perpetual Advent. And this Advent of Christ in the Church is one in which each of us must insert ourselves. If it differs from that of the Jews (in which everything is already given), it is not yet the definitive Advent, because everything that has substantially been given must yet be progressively assimilated. This second Advent, which is a time of personal sanctity and missionary extension, is ordered towards the third and final Advent.

III. The Third Advent: Christ's Return

The third Advent awaits the day in which Christ's action, begun by him and continued through the Church, will be consummated by his return. The second coming of Christ will essentially be the resounding in the whole of the cosmos of what was inwardly accomplished in God's children. "The whole of creation waits with eager expectation for the revelation of God's children" (Rom. 8:19). It does not wait for the existence of God's children, for we are already the children of God; but it awaits their manifestation. In other words, it awaits the day in which the divine power frees humanity from all suffering, from all weeping (Rev. 7:17), and from all slavery (Eph. 2:1-10), which endure even after souls have been freed from their sins.

We must thus try, through prayer, to enter into the great movement of God's action in history, in order to participate more deeply in this inner waiting for the coming of Christ in us, and also to participate more deeply in the missionary desire for the unfolding of his mystery in every nation. This is the profound meaning of the mystery of Christ's blood and passion.

CHAPTER TWO

The Evangelical Spirit
of Humility

Chapter 6 of St. Paul's Letter to the Galatians is a call at once to humility and to love, which are closely related to each other. We are able to draw three ideas from this: "Bear one another's burdens, and you will thus fulfill Christ's teaching" (6:2). "Make no mistake, God is not ridiculed," for he judges us in truth (6:7). "While we still have the time [that is, on this earth] let us continue to do the good" (6:9).

This remarkable text from St. Paul is one of those in whose light we ought to examine ourselves, allowing the spirit of the text, which is one of goodness, of kindness, of benevolence, and of the peace of Christ, to penetrate into our lives. Not only does the Lord teach us the spirit of humility, but the spirit of humility, moreover, is one of the essential characteristics of Christ: "Come to me, all you who labor and are burdened, and I will give you rest. Take my yoke upon you and follow my teachings, for I am meek and humble of heart, and you will find rest for your souls" (Matt. 11:28-30). "Have among you the same attitude which is that of the Son of God: He, though he was in the form of God, did not jealously grasp at equality with God. Rather, he emptied himself, taking the form of a slave, and became similar to men. Being in the form of a man, he humbled himself even further, becoming obedient to death, even death on a cross!" (Phil. 2:5). A whole ensemble of attitudes, which are very intimately related to the essence of the Christian attitude, are to be found in these texts.

Each of the Christian virtues is a mystery that we must allow the Holy Spirit to elucidate for us. All of the virtues are ambiguous and are subject to various perversions. Thus we could misinterpret the virtue of poverty either by taking it in a sense that is too material — by identifying it with the privation of goods — or in a sense that is too spiritual, making it something so internal that it never manifests itself externally! There is less danger of illusion with the virtue of charity, unless it is that we confuse pity — the heart's natural inclination — with Christian charity, which is something very demanding. Graham Greene has said some scathing things in this regard.

Humility is one of the most dangerous virtues because it can be moved in the direction of our natural inclinations, and we must thus be wary of this. Hence, a certain kind of self-effacement, and a certain kind of passivity, are perversions of humility; they can be a lack of courage to affirm ourselves when charity requires precisely this.

- Let us no longer confuse humility with the temptation to avoid an action that would be appropriate just because we wish to keep from taking pride in something good. We must learn to give primacy to the objective value of things much more than to their subjective effects. If it is something useful that God asks of us or that the service of others requires, what does it matter if we take a certain pride in it or a certain humiliation?

- Humility can also move in the direction of our fears, of the difficulties we may have in interacting with others, of the fear that we have of imposing ourselves on others. Fear makes us withdraw into ourselves. Yet we must have the courage to confront others, we must learn to risk their rebuffs and not participate in these fears, which often have at their basis a self-love or a certain dread of being misjudged or misunderstood. This form of shielding ourselves from the demands of love is in opposition to the humility which, like all Christian virtues, expresses itself through struggles. Authentic humility is found more in action than in withdrawal, and in the failures action entails.

Having denounced the dangers of humility, we will now discuss the different levels of humility. The most profound level is Christ's humility, which is a very great mystery.

I. The Humility of the Sinner

The first level of humility, the most obvious one, is accepting and acknowledging that we are sinners, repenting, and confessing our misery. This humility is absolutely necessary. Throughout the Gospels it is presented as the very condition for grace: "I have not come for the righteous [the Pharisees, those who believe they are righteous when in fact everyone is a sinner], but for sinners" (Matt. 8:13). The Gospels show us that it is the humble admission of sin that opens the heart to grace. For example, recall those beautiful stories of Mary Magdalene at Jesus' feet: "Your sins are forgiven [. . .] her many sins have been forgiven because she has shown great love" (Luke 7:47-48); and of the Prodigal Son: "Father, I have sinned against heaven and against you, and I am no longer worthy to be called your son" (Luke 15:18). We discover these same words, which are an evangelical combination of humility and trust, when we ourselves are moved by grace, and we confess our misery to the Father who loves us; and the very act of humbly acknowledging our guilt is already to be forgiven.

This conversion of the heart distinguishes itself from all forms of self-justification. To be humble means first not wanting to be in the right over against God. Not trying to prove ourselves right is already the beginning of prayer. We have the tendency to arrange everything according to our own point of view, to be in charge of our own lives, when we ought to allow God to arrange our lives and thereby to permit the Holy Spirit to work in us and to bring us into harmony with God's plan for us. This humility is the first grace that brings us to acknowledge that we have made mistakes and that we have followed paths that are not God's. It is a grace to know that we are sinners.

"Righteous men do not get mixed up with grace," Péguy says. A certain good conscience, a certain claim of righteousness, and a certain form of virtue close us to grace. There is immediately a sort of pharisaism in this conformism, a certain "worthiness" that is not authentic love. We must shed these scales in order to bare our hearts so that we consent to be judged by Christ and in his light. That is why there are virtuous people that are not touched by grace and, conversely, great sinners whom grace reaches profoundly.

II. The Humility of the Creature

The humility of the creature means acknowledging ourselves as creatures, accepting ourselves in all aspects, with all of our limitations. Here we touch upon many aspects of our spiritual life. "If anyone thinks he is something when he is nothing, he deludes himself" (Gal. 6:3). While we cannot put on an act with God, with other people we are always required to play a role to some degree because of social conventions. It is a false excuse and a false humility to avoid preaching the virtues to others that we do not practice ourselves. It would be insincere to propose ourselves as examples. Rather, we are to preach what Christ taught. When I preach, I proclaim that God judges us all, with myself at the front.

To ask things of others that we ourselves are incapable of can sometimes be an obligation of our apostolate or education. This form of humility manifests itself in various ways: to live more in what is than in what seems is an essential law of the spiritual life; to live more in God's eyes than in the eyes of others. The value that God gives things is the value they truly have. Quite often, however, we live according to how we wish to appear in the eyes of others. We become worried about what they might think or say about us, and through this we become insincere. We are led to act more according to what others expect from us than according to who we really are. We tend to play a different role when we are with our friends, with our parents, in our professional environment, etc.

This concern for appearance is one of the principal obstacles to meditation, silence, and prayer; for when we then find ourselves alone, face to face with ourselves, we ruminate over our disappointments and wounded self-love, or we dwell in self-satisfaction and complacency. What a burdening of our interior lives! The silence that is required for our peace with God is difficult to acquire under these conditions. Humility, thus, opposes itself to vanity.

We may be tempted to do something quickly or poorly when we are alone. This is true of prayer. If we were truly convinced that what matters in prayer is to be seen by the Father, we would pray in our rooms with as much perfection and as much respect as we do in church; this is one of the great secrets to humility and peace: "When you pray, go into your room and shut the door, and your Father who sees in secret will repay you" (Matt. 6:6). This is true also of the services we perform. Let us learn to love hidden services in spite of our tendency to prefer services that would give us a certain glory or advantage.

To accept and to desire to see the truth about ourselves — that is, to accept our own limitations, whether they be those of our minds, our hearts, our emotions, or our health — is a good attitude to learn. There are radically false attitudes as well. Certain people live in a continual attitude of rebellion, refusing to see themselves as they are, refusing to accept some of their limitations, and are therefore perpetually unhappy. We must constantly recall St. Paul's remarks on the charisms. These remarks, incidentally, come just before his words about love: "Are all apostles? Are all prophets? Are all doctors? Are all teachers? Do all have gifts of healing? Do all speak in tongues? Do all interpret?" (1 Cor. 12:29-30).

One thing alone matters in life, the depth of our love; and this is unconditional. There are poor people that are filled with the wonders of love. And Our Lord warns us that "it is more difficult for a rich man to enter into the kingdom of heaven than for a camel to pass through the eye of a needle" (Matt. 19:24). Let us not forget that being rich does not mean merely having a lot of money; there are also the riches of intelligence, beauty, character, and reputation. And every form of wealth carries by itself a certain temptation. If we can make a problematic use of our poverty, we can also make a problematic use of our wealth. What matters is not the unequal distribution of talents, but what we make of them.

One form of being rich is refusing poverty: being attached to something we do not have, a fact that renders us doubly unhappy and makes it difficult for us to share what we do have. There are people who possess great gifts — gifts of the heart, for example — who will not accept the lack of other gifts. They are haunted by the fact that they may possess less intelligence than those who are brilliant. This rejection of reality creates certain delusions: we become the person in our dreams that we wish we could be in reality. We must strive to recover for our real lives, humble as they may be, the energies we waste in our dreams. The smallest degree of real love, the smallest amount of real effectiveness is worth all of our dreams put together; they have a great value, placing us on the path toward the absolute and engaging us in the real work of God and the service of others.

All of this is important for the choice we make for the direction of our lives and for our vocations. May we learn to give ourselves entirely to that for which we were created, casting aside all vain regrets. May we learn to bury ourselves in the task at hand, giving it all our attention, and removing ourselves from anything that would distract, agitate, or worry us. "If anyone thinks he is something when he is nothing, he deludes himself. May each person examine his own work, and then he will have something to boast about with regard to him alone, and not with regard to someone else; for each person will have his own burden to carry" (Gal. 6:3-4).

In our relationships with others, humility consists in not comparing ourselves with them, not wanting to be better than they are, accepting

81

their qualities, and trying to rid ourselves of that little pang of anguish called envy when we encounter certain values in others that we do not ourselves possess. A certain spirit of ownership and pride causes us to suffer when we discover something good in other people; whereas the spirit of the gospel, the perfection of love, rejoices in all that is good even when others have things that we do not have, and desires the growth and success of all people. St. Benedict has explained that the condition for interior peace and humility is a reciprocal acceptance that consists in not comparing what is in us with what is in others. God gives each person what he or she needs; let us accept from God's hands in thanksgiving what he gives us. God loves us for what we are; he desires us such as we are, according to our own paths. Let us consent to enter more deeply into this path in order to become the masterpieces that God wishes to make of us.

Being humble means accepting reprimands and correction. Our true friends are those who help us to be and to live in truth. Those who flatter us, deceive us. If other people do not tell us the truth, we risk living in illusion; for other people often see us better than we see ourselves, both in what is good and in our defects. Among brothers and sisters in Christ, people should love each other sufficiently to correct each other in mutual affection and trust. This is what St. Paul calls fraternal correction. It is a great form of humility that may, of course, cause us pain. But it is also an aid in performing the services in the body of Christ that we are actually competent to perform. May our mutual striving for truth and reality take place in an environment of optimism and joy, for each of us is something wonderful in the eyes of God.

III. The Humility of Christ

This third form of humility is the most mysterious and the most profound. "He, though he was in the form of God, did not jealously grasp at equality with God. Rather, he emptied himself, taking the form of a slave" (Phil. 2:5). The example of humility given to us by

Christ does not consist in not being what one is, but in lowering oneself below what one is. There are two aspects to this humility of Christ.

First, there is the acceptance of being forgotten, misunderstood, and abused. Thus Fr. de Foucauld strove for a state of abjection in order to imitate Christ, who suffered from being scorned and forgotten. Thus the Christian fools in Russia, whose somewhat bizarre vocation was to be mocked and ridiculed, sought to attain a certain conformity to the insulted and ignored Christ. However, we do not all have to strive for these sorts of things. These are inspirations that the Holy Spirit planted in the hearts of certain saints, a St. Francis of Assisi, or a Fr. de Foucauld. In fact, by measuring our basic attitudes with those of Christ, we risk certain perversions: it is possible to be gravely deluded in the cultivation of humiliations; it is possible that there could be, in this, a certain psychological perversion, a certain indulgence in masochism.

On the other hand, when we encounter humiliations, failures, and misunderstandings without having sought them, we must learn to accept them. Now most of us are terribly attached to our reputations, and when we discover that someone has been speaking badly of us, we have a tendency to react with violence and with an instinctive vengeance. If, in these situations, we recall Christ before the Sanhedrin — as the friends of Christ do — we will understand that the cross of Christ consists not only in physical suffering but in being scorned as Christ was scorned. People have said much about the physical suffering of Christ during his passion, but Our Lord's worst suffering was due to his being degraded by the crowds of Galilee by whom he loved to be loved, as every person loves to be loved. Being rejected by one's community can be the most tragic thing in a person's life. Our Lord was placed among criminals. Souls formed in the Gospel seek this humility of Christ in humiliation; it is what St. Ignatius called the third degree of humility.

The humility of Christ also means that we take the lowest place in order to make ourselves servants. The abbé Huvelin said of Our Lord: "He took the lowest place to such an extent that no one could lift him from it." He who is Lord made himself a servant: "If I, who am your Master and Lord, have made myself your servant by washing your feet, so too must you become the servants of one another" (John 13:14). "He who exalts himself shall be humbled, and he who humbles himself shall be exalted," he says in the parable of the wedding banquet (Luke 14:11). The Lord cast off his dignity as Lord in order to come and serve us who are sinners.

Here we touch upon an essential element in the spirit of the gospel, something very important with respect to the Church's hierarchy: bishops experience the danger of appearing more as masters than as servants. The whole of the hierarchy of the Church is essentially ordered to service and can justify itself only as service. When we become attached to dignity for its own sake, and not for the fact that it is a service, it becomes tainted. The call to command is a call to greater service and greater humility.

"Let us bear one another's burdens" (Gal. 6:2). Let us relieve our sisters and brothers of their burdens, as they relieve us of ours, serving each other in every sphere, never becoming afraid of rendering others the humble services that compelled the saints to care for the sick, the lepers, etc. The first thing Mauriac did when he returned to a more fervent practice of the faith was to visit a poor family, as if an inner instinct instructed him that in order to become a disciple of Christ, one must begin by serving others.

Christ's humility, which is love, brought him to descend toward the lowly, not because the lowly had some special value, but to look for the one who was lost in order to help him raise himself up. Let us therefore avoid indulging ourselves with dreams of grandeur, but rather enter willingly into humble thoughts. The Holy Spirit brings us to understand all of these things, and this can break the chains that bind us. The Spirit is freedom, and we are still held captive by many bonds that freeze in us the spontaneity of the gift of love. We ask Our Lord to free us a little more from all forms of slavery, so that the gift of ourselves, the gift of love for God and for others, may, according to Christ and his example, develop in us more freely, more spontaneously, and more generously.

CHAPTER THREE

Redemption: The Center
of the Trinitarian Plan

The mystery of redemption is the center of the Trinitarian plan. Its source is the Father's love for us, it is accomplished through the mission of the Son, and it is fulfilled in us through the gift of the Holy Spirit.

Redemption is the work of the Trinity coming to gather up the whole of creation. From this perspective, we can see the profound unity of God's plan, centered on the blood of Christ. If creation itself is a work of the Trinity, redemption is the greatest of these works. It is the Son's mission to gather up all that the Trinity created in order to bring it to its completion. It is important, as we meditate on the mystery of Christ's passion, not to become fixed on its sensible and affective aspects, but through faith to reach the mystery of the work God accomplished through it, the work that forms the center and summit of his plan.

In the Letter to the Ephesians (1:3-14), we see the successive roles of the Father, the Son, and the Holy Spirit. Here we see God's plan as it unfolds in three moments: first, the preparation for Christ's work in the eternal plan of the Father; next, its realization in the person and mission of Christ; and finally, its fulfillment by the Spirit working in the Church, and guiding God's plan to its completion.

This remarkable vision, which contains the mystery of the Trinity, reveals itself in three moments: the moment of the Father, which is essentially the time of the Old Testament; the moment of the Son, which is essentially the time of the Gospel; and the moment of the Spirit, which is essentially the time of the Church.

I. The Preexistence of God's Plan in the Love of the Father

The preexistence of the whole of God's plan in the Father's love and in the eternal wisdom of the Trinity is the very meaning that creation has always had for God. It is predestined. St. Paul's use of the word *predestination* does not carry the same meaning that it did in the controversy over grace and freedom; rather, it means that a thing is "present in divine wisdom before its actualization in time." In other words, everything has been desired by God in his eternal love before becoming progressively actualized in the economic order.

The Fathers of the Church have also spoken of the preexistence of the Church. She appears in the Pastor of Hermas as an old woman: "The Church existed before the creation of the world, and it is for her that the world was created." This is what gives the Church her full dimension. When we think about this period of history, and realize that the Church was made up of only twelve men and a few hundred disciples, we recognize the boldness of this vision of faith which sees in this small group of people that for which the whole world was made. It is with these same eyes of faith that we are able to see, in Christ crucified and scorned by the world, the word of God accomplishing the central event of history. Faith means believing that God has intervened in human history, and prayer means exploring these divine works with the eyes of faith in order to try to understand their content and meaning. It is thus that redemption first appears in the eternal plan of the Father: "By his love, God has predestined us to become his adopted sons" (Eph. 1:5).

God created us only so that we could share in his joy. If it were not true that God created us so that we could share eternally in his life, existence would have absolutely no meaning; the world would be absurd. It is only in faith in the intentions of God's love that the world finds its meaning. The world has no other justification than its having been destined in Christ for divine beatitude. This is the response to all those who would object that "a good God would not have been able to create a world so full of misery and suffering." St. Paul responds that it is through this that God seeks to build — and will irrevocably and ultimately succeed in building — the city of God in which his children will be bathed in the light of the Trinity.

God's plan has crossed through the drama of evil and sin. And if evil and sin are able to hinder this plan, they will nevertheless fail to foil it. God, who introduced the first man and the first woman into paradise — that is, into his beatitude — pursues his goal through the drama of sin by introducing the sacrifice of his Son. The mystery of creation becomes the mystery of redemption because of this conflict between love's intentions and the resistance of evil. Through redemption, the plan of love triumphs in this confrontation, and evil is destroyed.

Far from finding obstacles in the mysteries of evil, sin, and freedom, our faith situates itself precisely within them: Christ intervenes at a level that we are unable to reach ourselves, a level that exceeds us and is beyond our grasp. It is in the depths of our existence, within the mysteries of sin and the resurrection, that God works out his plan.

The goal of the Father's eternal love is the city of his adopted children, to which he wishes to communicate the fullness of his life, thus revealing the glory of his grace: "The glory of God is the living man," St. Irenaeus says. What glorifies God is the splendor and grandeur of his work, because in this city of God's children, in the mystery of grace, the grandeur of what God has made finally appears. As we contemplate the beauty of creation, we come to understand God's grandeur because all things refer to him. At the same time, humanity's grandeur is capable of masking God's grandeur from us — this is the temptation of the modern world. Nevertheless, it is through humanity's grandeur that God's grandeur is revealed to us, to the extent that we understand that everything great in humankind comes from God. This is what we respond to Protestants when they reproach us for giving too much glory to the Blessed Virgin. In reality, when we glorify the Virgin, we are withholding nothing from God or Christ, because we confess that everything she possesses is a free gift from God. And the more that we see the Blessed Virgin as great and preeminent among God's children, the more we understand the greatness of God, who is able to create such a miracle. The Immaculate Conception is the eruption of the glory of grace.

Failing to understand what God wishes to make of us, a materialist may reject the Creator of all of these failed lives we lead that ultimately fade into nothingness. Not understanding God's plan for the world, an atheist may legitimately commit blasphemy. But the world is nevertheless justified, and God is glorified when we acknowledge ourselves as predestined in Christ to be God's children, when we realize that through his gratuitous love, God has called us to eternal life.

Christ reveals to us what God desires to create. This is why we must give glory to his grace and glorify the Father of Our Lord Jesus Christ who has given us such love, who at every moment arouses in us the life of his Word in order to communicate to us the fullness of his life. As yet we know very little about this life, but it nevertheless already animates us and will one day blossom into the fullness of beatitude and eternal joy. As St. Leo said, "Ah! Christian, if you only knew your dignity and the grandeur of your vocation." Yes, then we would be capable of confronting the atheism, rationalism, and scepticism that we find around us today with a joyous, peaceful, and confident certitude that truly bears witness to the Father, who is so misunderstood and ridiculed.

II. The Accomplishment of God's Plan
by the Blood of Christ

The Letter to the Ephesians brings us into the center of the redemptive mystery: "In Him [Christ] we have redemption by his blood, the forgiveness of sins" (1:7). Because the confrontation with the mystery of evil and sin is at the heart of the fulfillment of God's plan, God's work does not consist simply in communicating grace, but also in destroying evil, in freeing humankind from what holds him captive. That is why God's action in the Word will take the form of the mystery of the Cross. The aspect of sacrifice in Christ's work has as its object the glorification of the Father, who has been abused by sin, and also the victory over death. He triumphs over death by accepting enslavement by it so that humanity can be set free. This is the whole meaning of the death and resurrection of Christ, who descends into the most inaccessible depths of suffering and so destroys evil at its roots. There is but one solution to the mystery of evil: the triumphant Cross of Christ.

Every explanation becomes unbearable in the face of suffering; every human effort becomes ridiculous in the face of evil. We are unable to bring consolations or explanations to someone in the midst of suffering; all we can do is try to relieve some of his or her suffering. Jesus Christ alone brings victory over the suffering of bodies and souls. As a modern novel puts it, "One word alone is possible, that which proclaims the resurrection of the body; all other words are just so much babbling." We believe that Christ resolves the whole human drama because he alone reaches into its ultimate depths. We must avoid leaving Christianity on the surfaces; it is neither a system of morality, nor a social order, nor a system of metaphysics. Rather, it is the fact that what is inaccessible to humankind, what reveals the very mystery of his existence as neither morality nor sociology could do, has been achieved by the word of God. We can criticize all philosophical systems — like Marxism, for example — of being superficial, because they fail to reach to the roots of the problem of human suffering into which Jesus Christ alone has descended. The moment that Christ descended into the abyss of hell is the most important moment in history.

We are called to make an authentic act of faith in order to see in Christ's passion his confrontation with the mystery of evil and to affirm that evil is definitively vanquished by Christ on the cross, that through him we have been liberated from evil and have already become God's children. St. Paul gives us the full dimensions of the redemptive act when he says, "At the fullness of time the Father has reunited all things in Jesus Christ, those in heaven and those on earth" (Eph 1:10). To this phrase, we may add another from the Letter to the Colossians: "God desired all the fullness to dwell in him; and through him wished to reconcile all things to himself, those in heaven and those on earth, making peace through the blood of his cross" (Col. 1:19-20).

The drama of human history is revealed through the mystery of his blood. The book of Revelation speaks of the scroll sealed with seven seals that no one can open (meaning not only that no one can explain, but also that no one can reveal them). The Angel says to John: "Behold the one who will open the seal," and "I saw a lamb standing in their midst that had been sacrificed" (Rev. 5:1-6). It is Jesus, the sacrificial Lamb, who reveals the destiny of humanity that had remained sealed until his coming, and no one before him had been able to reveal it.

The Fathers of the Church saw, in the four dimensions of the cross, a sign that redemption is extended universally. St. Paul had sketched this idea of the cosmic cross in speaking of the four dimensions of Christ's love: its height, width, length, and depth (Eph. 3:18). As St. Irenaeus put it, "Christ on the Cross, through his outstretched arms, seeks to embrace all people, from the East to the West." In this there is a sort of double reconciliation. On one hand, there is the reconciliation of humanity with God and with the angels (the vertical dimension); and on the other hand, because humanity is reconciled with God, there is the reconciliation among people (the horizontal dimension). Our sign of the cross, rather than being a mechanical thing, reminds us that the love for God and the love for our brothers and sisters are absolutely joined, and signifies the reconciliation of all things with God and in Christ.

III. The Action of the Holy Spirit

What the Father has eternally foreseen, what Christ has accomplished in his flesh in his victory over sin and reconciliation of all things with himself, the Holy Spirit sent by the Father and the Son at Pentecost begins to actualize mysteriously in our poor hearts. The Holy Spirit dwelling within us, the Spirit of the seal with which we were marked on the day of our baptism, begins to awaken in us the eternal life as children of God that was envisioned by the Trinity.

Perhaps no other text states as forcefully the presence in us of the Trinity as this one: "You have been marked with the seal of the promised Holy Spirit [in Baptism] which is the first installment of our inheritance, awaiting the full redemption of those God acquired for himself to the praise of his glory" (Eph. 1:13-14). Through this text we see the grandeur of the Blessed Trinity, to whom all glory and honor is due, because it is through this marvelous plan that we understand how great and worthy of our love the Trinity is, who in the Father conceived of this plan of love, who in the Son's sacrifice made love manifest, who in the gift of the Spirit — the love itself of the Father and the Son — already brings us to live by the life of love as children of God. It is the Holy Spirit filling our hearts who says "Abba, Father" (Gal. 4:6). Through the Spirit, we are children of God and other Christs. The spiritual life is the life of the Spirit, who groans in us in eager expectation of the full redemption of our bodies, the total liberation from all limitations that weigh on us and from which we know we will one day be freed (cf. Rom. 8:19-22).

Each time we meditate on these great texts we must ask God to deliver us more fully to the plan of the Trinity so that God can work his miracles in us and, by introducing us into the Trinitarian plan, can make us his servants.

PART FOUR

The Growth of the Church

CHAPTER ONE

The Spirit of Mission

Here we will examine in succession the foundations of the spirit of mission, and then the concrete expressions it ought to take.

I. The Foundations of the Spirit of Mission

Mission has its origin in prayer. What distinguishes the missionary attitude from other attitudes toward people is that it carries a religious dimension. There are many reasons, for example, why a person might be interested in the Arabic world, whether they be cultural (the attraction of Arabic humanism), economic (the problem of underdeveloped countries), or reasons of mission (the Islamic world not having the full knowledge and faith of the true God).

Prayer is related to mission because it is to the extent that we have discovered who God is and how much a knowledge and love of God is constitutive of a comprehensive humanism and a full and complete existence that we suffer from, and are struck by, situations in which God is not known or loved. At the basis of the missionary attitude lies a certain scandal with respect to the reversal of values in which God holds such a small place in people's various preoccupations while other things hold such a large one. A recognition

95

of a certain absence of God in the world is part of the missionary attitude. As we become aware of our relationship to God and of the vital revelation of God given to us in Christ — that is, of the mystery of the Trinity — we suffer to see that people ignore God altogether (the world of atheism), or that they fail to see the full truth of God (pagan religions, Islam, and Judaism).

To the extent that we come to see how much God deserves to be loved, we desire that God be loved by others as well; and we suffer to see God remain unknown or unrecognized. Thus, with an ardent missionary zeal, St. Paul burned with a desire to make the true God known to all people, because he knew, as St. Irenaeus said, that "man exists in order to see God."

There is therefore no opposition between contemplation and mission. The notion that there would be, and that one would have to choose between them, is absurd. On the contrary, mission appears as the self-unfolding of contemplation. The great missionaries were first great contemplatives. St. Francis of Assisi was the hermit of Alverne before he began to spread his evangelical message. St. Ignatius was a contemplative, living the life of a hermit at Manrese and Montserrat, the life of a monk in the desert, before feeling a desire to share with others what he had lived. And conversely, as one among those who are contemplative "by profession," St. Bernard often left his monastery. He himself said, "I am the chimera of the century, neither monk nor layman; when I am in the monastery I burn with the zeal for souls, and I have only one desire, to go and preach. As soon as I am outside, I feel homesick for my monastery and for solitude with God alone." St. Teresa of Avila spent her time traveling the roads of Spain.

To be sure, with a contemplative, this missionary zeal can in many cases be expressed only on the level of prayer, but one would not imagine that a contemplative would not be devoured by a zeal to share with others the love she or he has for God. The idea that a contemplative would be someone perpetually lost in celestial space without any connection with the earth would be absolutely false from the perspective of Christian prayer. Christian prayer is not in the slightest degree a form of escape. On the contrary, it brings us ever more deeply into human life. It strives to bring the movement of God's love, the Spirit, into the thick and heavy dough of human existence in order to make it rise. To experience this, we must first be grasped by the Spirit; we must first be filled with the life of the Spirit. Conversely, we could not imagine an authentic apostle or an authentic missionary whose apostolic spirit does not immerse him or her in God's intimacy. What differs between the two are the modes of prayer. There are modes of prayer that work through separation and disengagement with images and concepts. There are also modes of prayer that work more through symbols, images, and concrete realities.

A saint is always someone who has a sense of God's grandeur, who has found joy in God, and who, filled with this love, desires to communicate it and share it, just as one would desire to speak of whatever it is that fills one's heart. If we do not speak enough about God, it is because our hearts are not sufficiently filled with him. A heart filled with God speaks of God without effort, whereas it often takes effort for us because our hearts are not sufficiently enflamed. There are monks whose hearts are filled with God, there are apostles whose hearts are filled with God, and there are humble women whose hearts are filled with God, who cannot help speaking of God because it is he who fills their hearts. There are mothers whose hearts are filled with God, and there are children whose hearts are filled with God.

Obviously, there is no need to wait until our hearts are completely filled with God in order to speak of him, because we could end up waiting indefinitely. There is a sort of mutual causality here. Interaction with souls often becomes a call to prayer. God attracts us to souls, and souls attract us to God through a reciprocal movement. Priests often have this experience: there are confessions in which the confessor comes out more converted than the one confessing. When we touch upon the power of grace in the soul of a sinner who opens him- or herself up with a total humility, we have no other need for proofs of God's existence. When the holy soul of a monk simply recounts a little of what God has done for him, we feel a wonder at God's marvels in our hearts.

There is also a mutual causality between prayer and mission. When we have spoken to others of God, and when we have had this concern for mission, we experience the need to pray more deeply. At the eve of certain days in which we have experienced the weight of souls, we feel a need to entrust this crushing responsibility to God. And so, in the simple and silent relationship between a soul and her God, everything is shared: God hears us, and we hear God. At these moments, our hearts open themselves up and become fully pervaded by grace. We must experience this profoundly and become aware of the danger of a certain activism in our apostolate in order to maintain the primacy of the spiritual orientation and the primacy of the desire to communicate God to others.

Without minimizing the duties of corporal mercy, which today are expressed primarily through social service, international service, or various forms of aid to underdeveloped countries, a Christian must never forget that the first form of suffering is spiritual suffering. The spirit of mission is a form of charity that opens us to the works of spiritual mercy. It is an awareness of the suffering of souls.

Our age tends to be more sensitive to bodily suffering. The great movement today in the battle against the world's suffering and the feeling of social responsibility are authentic expressions of evangelical charity. The Church is discovering this more and more: within this order, Paul VI represents a step further with respect to John XXIII. Paul VI established the urgency of the Christian's social duty because Christians generally know the social doctrine of the Church, but very few put it into practice in any way that requires sacrifices of them.

The duty of temporal service, considered as a Christian service, is gradually increasing in importance and helps us to integrate politics into morality. The fact that it is through service in the political, social, or international order that gospel charity expresses itself is one aspect of the transformation of the contemporary Christian. The effect that John XXIII's teachings had is a sign of how sensitive modern people are to the inseparability of evangelical and political morality.

Having said this, it would be a mistake to make corporal mercy the essential aspect of the Christian's mission, because the first thing Christians must bring to others is God. To act otherwise would imply that spiritual suffering is less significant than physical suffering, when in fact it is the most significant. It is enough to have seen people in the midst of suffering to realize that the sufferings of the spirit are infinitely worse than physical sufferings, because they reach into the most profound depths of a person. We all know sick people who, to the extent that their spiritual being is ultimately in harmony with the absolute, continue to be happy in the midst of their pain. The opposite, however, is never the case. There are an infinite number of people who suffer morally and spiritually. The curé of Ars, for example, was sensitive to sickness, suffering, and spiritual wounds. When a person arrived at his confessional, he would read their hearts: "It was as if rays of grace shot forth from his hands to heal wounds." Just like Christ, the curé of Ars laid his hands on sick souls and healed them. Throughout the centuries, the great apostles have been great healers of souls.

Christ's charity was situated on the same level. In the Gospels, we recall that every time someone asks Christ for material services — the newlyweds at Cana who had no more wine for their thirsty guests, for example — the Lord begins by refusing, saying he did not come for that, that he did not want to be merely an instrument for the solution to worldly problems, since the very goal of his mission was to teach that the true problems are not worldly ones. Having said this, Christ transforms the water into wine, and multiplies the loaves — but only after having made it understood that this miracle was only a supplement!

This is the whole pedagogy of prayer. We always begin by asking God to solve our difficulties, until the day we understand that it would be a perversion of our relationship with God if we expected from him only the satisfaction of our worldly needs, when the most essential thing he has to bring us is the revelation of who he is in himself.

Having a missionary spirituality means also that we must maintain in ourselves a sense of the spiritual suffering at every level, that we must suffer more from it ourselves, experience a compelling concern, and yet refrain from participating in it. This is what people expect from the Church. An atheist will always be surprised if a Christian never speaks of anything but social organization or economic change, for he secretly expects something else from him. There is a sort of uncertainty in his heart, and, sometimes secretly, a desire: Christians who would never move on to this other level would disappoint him. An atheist expects the Christian to explain a little bit to him about the things of God, and if this Christian seems not to attach much importance to these things, if he seems to consider purely human problems to be the most urgent, the atheist is disappointed. In this sense, Christians often disappoint non-Christians.

What non-Christians reproach Christians for is not for being Christians, but for not being perfect. Undoubtedly, they sometimes exaggerate this or reproach them unjustly, because it is easy enough to criticize from the outside. Those who would wish every Christian to be a saint are unable to acknowledge the necessarily human part of the Church. But fundamentally the reproach is legitimate. Certain Christian writings, like those of Bernanos, reach atheists because they go straight to what is essential: the trinitarian and sacramental dimensions of the Christian life. This is what interests non-Christians, what they would like very much to understand, what they do not understand, what they would like someone to explain to them, and, above all, what they would like to experience themselves. Christians would be silly to "keep under the bushel basket" precisely what makes them interesting!

We, as Christians, do not have a monopoly on social service, nor on technological development, nor on solutions for world peace and hunger in underdeveloped countries. To a large extent, atheists are just as capable as Christians in solving these problems. But, in the total perspective, Christians are able to bring something that will always be lacking in purely technical solutions. With respect to technological development, we are, as the texts from Vatican II have said, in service of the human work with all people of goodwill without claims of having any privileges over them. A natural love for others is sometimes very deep in non-Christians, and Christians must make no claims of being "experts in the love of neighbor." The charity that the Holy Spirit pours into our hearts is a transformation of the love of neighbor, raising it above itself. But it is normal for many non-Christians to have as much love for their sisters and brothers and as much of a sense of solidarity as Christians do — and sometimes more.

It is important to see clearly what is irreplaceable in Jesus Christ: he liberates us from evil, spiritual suffering, sin, and death. Only Jesus can do this. People await this liberation eagerly, from the bottom of their hearts. Our mission is to proclaim and communicate it. To do so, we must possess a sense of the preeminent character of what Christ alone can bring. This is as true with respect to atheism as it is with respect to all non-Christian religions: there exists, in these religions, a sense of God and of the search for God; but Christ is the response to this search; and in this sense, there is no salvation outside of Jesus Christ.

The Incarnation is God's gesture of coming in order to liberate and save humanity. And this — which we may confess in the greatest humility — has nothing to do with us. We are the awed witnesses of something that has made us its beneficiaries; but others may also be its beneficiaries. We haven't the slightest monopoly on salvation, and it does not belong to us to the slightest degree. Salvation is an absolutely gratuitous gift for which we can only give thanks, but which is offered just as much to others. That is why there is no arrogance or pretension for a Christian in bearing witness to Jesus Christ.

Such is the meaning of spiritual suffering. It is connected with the spiritual life. All of the great saints, faced with the world of sin, have experienced a burning zeal to take the world's sins upon themselves, to free souls from this sin and spiritual suffering, and to help them become the "living" to a greater extent — and they have been great apostles along the paths of the world.

The ecclesial aspect of the spirit of mission is the one that is most being developed today. This aspect of universalism in the Church is an opening to the values possessed by others and an attempt to burst through whatever had been rigid in her own. From this point of view, it is essential to the spirit of mission to possess a sense of relative incarnations of Christianity and an opening to forms of incarnation other than our own, coming to acknowledge that Christianity is not identical with the form it has taken in the West.

We cannot insist enough on the fact that we must *receive* from others as much as we must *give* to them. We need to eliminate any residual spiritual colonialism from the spirit of mission. This is not easy, and it is far from being the case in a country like France. The majority of French Christians are deeply persuaded of the superiority of their Christianity over that of the Africans and would be scandalized if someone were to suggest that the latter would have something to bring them.

Nevertheless, the love of others does not mean that we must disparage ourselves; we must also love Western civilization and Christianity. It is unbearable to hear people say that there is no mysticism outside of India, when in France there are many remarkable mystics hidden in the contemplative life of the monastery. Similarly, an affinity for Semitic cultures does not preclude an appreciation for the Greek and Latin cultures. There is a certain way of glorifying the other that is unhealthy, for at its roots is a certain resentment. It is a way of criticizing our own culture. Thus we have Christians who admire everything done outside of the Church and have nothing but distrust and contempt for anything done within the Church. Sometimes it is necessary for unbelievers to reveal to believers the Church's beautiful social teachings.

We recall the word St. Paul uses in the Letter to the Galatians (6:10): *"Faciamus bonum ad omnes, maxime autem ad domesticos fidei"* (Let us do good unto others, above all to our brothers in the faith). The word *domestici* is a remarkable one. For the ancients, it meant "all those who participate in the *domus* (house)." Let us thus love those in our house. An authentic attitude would be one that, while enabling us to do justice to the greatness of Western Christianity and everything it has inspired, also brings us to love what our sisters and brothers in Africa and Asia have achieved or are able to achieve. We have as much to receive from them as they do from us, and we must be even more careful since their creations, being more recent and therefore more fragile, could easily be crushed by us with our obvious superiorities. Here we touch upon some extremely important and delicate problems in the dialogue with our sisters and brothers from other cultures and with our non-Christian brothers and sisters. Our dialogue with the Africans, for example, can be rendered difficult by the sensitivity and vulnerability that is often exposed.

These sorts of difficulties are the daily bread of missionary dialogue. They may often take on a quality of acuteness; consequently, in order to discover an appropriate attitude, we must recall that receiving can be as great a form of love as giving. It is an illusion to believe that one can love only by giving: this would be to proclaim oneself rich and to affirm the other as poor. The object of this sort of charity will be humiliated by it, and it is a very serious wrong to humiliate a person. What is most sensitive in a person today is his or her feeling of worth and dignity: how many Africans have told us that the problem of Africa is the problem of the perpetual offense of human dignity! Knowing this helps us to understand how delicate our interaction with them is, how much tact is necessary, and how easily these hearts could close themselves off. There is, in this, a whole psychology to be learned.

II. Concrete Expressions of the Spirit of Mission

Formation in the dialogue with non-Christians is more than a matter of acquiring information. It is preparation for dialogue, which presupposes both self-knowledge — that is, a knowledge of Christianity in its depths — and knowledge of the other. Here again, we must react against a tendency to feel superior that causes those in the West to think it unnecessary to learn about other civilizations and religions, while thinking it normal that others would want to know about their own. This formation presupposes more than a relatively passive taking in of conferences; it requires personal work and real effort.

The non-Christians that we will most commonly encounter are those at the office, at the factory, and at school. Dialogue with these people necessitates that we engage the greatest problems of the modern world, most notably those of Marxism and atheism. It is not possible to dialogue with a Marxist if we Christians are not aware that the authentic dialogue takes place not only on the level of external problems, but also on the level of the fundamental reasons for which we reject Marxism in the name of a defense of humanity. In effect, it is not a matter of defending one position over against another, but of defending something which, for us, is vital. And we must therefore be capable of making this understood.

The ecumenical dialogue with the Protestant and Eastern Orthodox Churches will become more and more important after Vatican II. We must be able to explain to Protestants that we are not Protestants because we wish to keep the whole of Christ's message, and that we are certain that the institution of a hierarchy of living men is part of it, as an instrument for the transmission of Christ's sacraments and message, and as a place of divine action in our midst, in the sacramental efficacity and infallibility of the Tradition. Moreover, we must study what distinguishes Orthodox ecclesiology from Catholic ecclesiology in order to enable the members of the Catholic Church to dialogue with an Orthodox. The ignorance of Catholics with respect to the Eastern Church has always scandalized the Orthodox, who have always followed events in the Latin Church.

In a similar way, the Christian must study Islam, Judaism, and the religions of Asia and Africa.

Taking spiritual responsibility for others means keeping the non-Christian world and spiritual suffering present in our prayer. We must learn to deepen the specifically missionary form of prayer and liturgy. We might, for example, choose a particular intention each month to incarnate and give direction to this orientation. We must keep present the suffering of the non-Christian world in which we are immersed and make it a real concern, an "apostolic passion," as the father of the Grandmaison put it.

Making contact with non-Christians means not closing ourselves up within a Christian environment; rather, from where we are, we must seek to make contact and to create bonds of friendship with non-Christians. This is not easily done, because it is more pleasant for us to remain with our friends than to engage in conversation with a Communist comrade or a non-Christian colleague. Too often, the Christian community coincides with a certain sociological milieu. This is extremely serious because the Church then becomes a ghetto — that is, one milieu among others — and the universal scope of the message gets lost.

The reunion of Christians in the eucharistic community will be all the more intense if they will have been spread out among others the rest of the time. The eucharistic assembly takes on its full meaning when it gathers "those of the house," the sisters and brothers with whom we have all things in common, with whom we want to share everything, but with the goal of passing the message to those around us. The opportunities to do so are easily discovered and pursued. When leaving a faculty lecture, for example, instead of waiting for our friends and meeting up with them, we could notice the presence of a Muslim, a Vietnamese, or a non-Christian student, make contact, and exchange a few words with him or her. Admittedly, this would require sacrifices, but there is no missionary opening without sacrifices. In this regard, a real commitment to making contact and a preference for non-Christians is necessary. Here again, this is distinguished from the Catholic Action movement, whose primary goal is to invigorate Christian communities.

Formation and engagement are related. On the one hand, it is only when we are properly formed that we can validly engage with others; on the other hand, dialogue nourishes our research, because our knowledge of the other is made, not only through ties, but also through engagement with human beings. After having had a conversation with a Muslim student, we feel the need to take up a book in order to understand the five commandments he discussed. Human contacts incite curiosity, and, conversely, intellectual knowledge causes us to desire contact with people.

CHAPTER TWO

The Apostle's Mission as a Continuation of the Mystery of Christ

We will deepen what we have said previously about the missionary spirit by considering it on a more interior level as the continuation of the Mystery of Christ in the Church. St. Paul helps us here: we may reread, on this subject, the beautiful text from the Second Letter to the Corinthians (4:7-15), in which the apostle expresses his feelings with regard to the little community at Corinth, which he founded and which is disrupted by contrary opinions. Through this passage emerge the inward dispositions of a heart concerned with souls, a heart that loves them and that suffers from their infidelities and their imperfections, a heart that expresses this love with an overwhelming sincerity.

The apostle Paul appears here as one who is engaged in the battle begun in Christ that will continue until the end of time. The missionary spirituality is a participation in the continuing Mysteries of Christ, a confrontation with the world of sin, and a penetration of this world in a battle destined to bring the world to completion. The apostle carries on the three dimensions of the Mystery of Christ.

I. The Incarnation

The Word of God comes looking for people because he loves them. The point of departure for any apostolate is to love as Christ loves; that is, with a love that achieves in the other what Christ loves in him. Such is the basic missionary attitude: to love in souls that which the Spirit tries to accomplish in them, to be in conspiracy with this action of the Spirit that seeks to make a masterpiece of each human soul.

Charity, in the biblical sense of the word, brings us to love others as persons and to work toward their spiritual fulfillment, bringing out what is best in them, encouraging every spark of love. It consists essentially in helping, as does the Holy Spirit (*Paraclete,* in fact, means "helper"). The Holy Spirit is the Paraclete insofar as he remains near us in order to support us, to help us, and to bring out the blossoming of everything good within us. Similarly, the gaze of love remains near others, seeing what is good in them, seeking to make it grow, occasionally making them aware that there is something better within them that they ignore, and helping them to discover the wonderful vocation that is their own.

This atheist comrade, this Communist colleague, this Muslim friend — each is loved by Christ and destined to share his life. The eyes of faith thus make us see and love in others that unique vocation to which all, without exception, are called. For there is not one single human being who is not destined, one day, to be transformed in Christ and to contemplate the Trinity. The missionary perspective anticipates the fulfillment of this vocation. Following the spirituality of St. John the Baptist, the missionary sees in others what they could be, though not yet are; and because he loves them, he desires to see them blossom fully into what God has destined them to be. It is not a question of bringing to others what they do not yet have, but of helping them to be what they already are by finding their vocation in Christ. It is not a question of making them like us, but of helping them to fully accomplish what they are called to be.

In each person, the grace of God is truly at work. And charity consists always in assisting the blossoming of souls. That is why charity is essentially kind, as St. Paul tells us in his beautiful eulogy of love: "Love is patient, love is kind, love is not puffed up with pride, love rejoices in truth . . . it excuses all things, it believes all things, it hopes all things, it encourages all things" (1 Cor. 13:4-7). The words "it hopes all things" express something essential: love, in effect, believes in the possibility for every human soul to achieve the fullness of his vocation. If Christians do not have a monopoly on human love, there is, nevertheless, a divine love that is properly Christian and irreplaceable, insofar as it reaches in the other the divine dimension that a purely human love cannot. This divine love is able to love more completely, more profoundly, more wholly, because it brings us to love in others that eternal part of themselves which they often ignore.

Charity is thus first this attachment to the marvelous creation of God in human souls that brings us to enter into the movement of creative love. God is life and seeks to bring about life. To love with a missionary love means to seek to bring about the fullness of life that is the blossoming of the life of grace, of the spiritual life in a soul. It is for this reason that we must love others with a love that does not stop at the exterior, but that reaches into the depths of their beings. This is what gives all Christian love its depth, whether it be the love between spouses or friends, or especially missionary love, insofar as it is a kind of anticipation, through love, of what does not yet exist.

God's love is creative. God does not love us because we are good; we are good because God loves us. His love is the source of our goodness. In the same way, what is remarkable in the mystery of the Visitation is Mary's anticipation, which goes beyond Elizabeth. She "anticipates," and her approach inspires in the infant dwelling in Elizabeth's womb the divine grace that causes him to rejoice.

Divine love is always anticipatory, and missionary love is essentially anticipatory. It does not do to wait for non-Christians to come to us; it is up to us to go to them, because before we were Christians, Christ left his Father's house in order to come to us through love.

The gesture by which we go to look for what is lost, the love by which we love Christ in others, anticipates this presence of Christ that is sometimes still to be achieved in them. How differently we would see our Muslim or atheist friends if we were to see them and love them thus in the light of Christ! Our apostolate would become more intelligent; it would not be proselytizing, but simply desiring that the one we love be enriched by every gift capable of bringing him or her the fullness of joy.

II. Participation in Redemption

In his Incarnation, Christ collides with the world of sin. Love collides with rejection, with evil. It thus becomes a redemptive love, that is, a battle against the forces of evil. In an atheist, for example, there are two realities: there is first the soul created by God and loved by Jesus Christ; and, on the other hand, there exists something that is not at all lovable, that is even hateful, something to which we can by no means become partisan: the error that holds him captive. We must be very careful — because it is an easy pitfall — that our love for non-Christians, for atheists and the values they hold, not become partisan to what is in error in them, because in this way we would be betraying them, and we would no longer be loving them truly. We must in no way become partisan to anything that is contrary to Christ — neither atheism, nor Hinduism, nor Islam. To the same extent that we ought to be open to any positive reality, we must avoid being partisan to error. Does a mother love the failures and shortcomings in her child? No, on the contrary, she suffers from them. Similarly, to the degree that we love a person, we suffer profoundly from the presence of evil and sin in him or her.

Mission thus appears as a conflict with the forces of evil: it is a spiritual combat that is not played out primarily externally, but rather inwardly. Christ — and this is an essential aspect of his mystery — has confronted evil in its totality. *"Mors et vita duello conflixere mirando"* (Death and Life are engaged in an incredible duel) — an extraordinary duel according to the beautiful expression from the Paschal Sequence. St. Paul tells us that this battle between life and death continues in us: "we always carry in our body the death of Jesus, so that the life of Jesus may also be manifested in our body" (2 Cor. 4:10).

There is no mission without a passion. There is no mission without an apostle delivered over with Christ in this battle that is "bloodier than the battles of men," as Rimbaud said, in which the forces of good and evil confront each other. This explains the greater part of the failures that accompany missionary activity, failures that we would be naive to deny. Failure, the fact of colliding with forces we do not succeed in overcoming, plays a part in the plan of redemption: it is the mystery of Christ who has saved the world — not by a triumph, but by a failure — because it is essentially in being broken against the forces of resistance, and in offering himself totally in a gesture of infinite love, that he has covered a multitude of sins. It is to this aspect of failure that St. Paul alludes when he says: "We are oppressed, but not crushed; in distress, but not in despair; persecuted, but not abandoned; struck down, but not lost; always carrying in our body the death of Jesus" (2 Cor. 4:8-9).

For St. Paul, all the obstacles he comes up against, the battles he fights to communicate the life of Jesus Christ, are the continuation in his body of the death of Jesus, the condition necessary so that the life of Jesus may be made manifest. This death points to life. St. Paul helps us to understand that the spiritual battle, and in particular the battle that makes up our spiritual life, is, to the extent that we confront all the forces opposed to it, to the extent that it is continually crossed with hardships, a battle for the redemption of the world.

The goal of the sacrifices that prayer demands of us is not only the success of our individual prayer life (that would not fully satisfy us and would not form us); but even more, they are a participation in the cosmic battle between Christ and the forces of evil. We engage these battles with all of our friends in the faith, and clusters of souls hang from our fidelities. When we have no desire to pray, the weight of these souls for which we are responsible helps us to hold firm.

This grants a meaning of love and redemption to the battle that makes up every spiritual life. In other words, if we have trouble praying or giving ourselves faithfully, it is not simply because the circumstances are not favorable, or because we do not have the time; but rather, on a more profound level, it is because of the spiritual effort as such that it costs us.

We have elsewhere remarked that the more progress we make in our spiritual life, the more temptations we experience. The greatest saints experience the greatest temptations, and the great temptations are those described by the great spiritual writers. Satan takes their bodies in hand because they are dangerous to him. Certain souls, peaceful at the beginning of their spiritual lives, become disturbed by temptations when they believe that they have made a little progress. And these temptations may be humiliating — temptations against purity, temptations of sensuality, hatred, and sloth. It is a mistake to think that saints are not tempted.

Sanctity is not some sort of safe haven where one comes to rest after the efforts of getting started. On the contrary, the more a saint advances in sanctity, the more his or her battle against the forces of evil grows. *The Life of St. Anthony* will remain the simple, picturesque, and continually valid masterpiece of these spiritual combats. To become a monk or nun in order to find peace or to escape responsibilities would be to delude oneself. One does not enter into the convent through fear of responsibilities or through despair of love — regardless of what some may think — but to be at the pitch of the spiritual battle for the salvation of souls. By entering a monastery, a monk knows that he exposes himself, that he throws a challenge to the forces of evil, and thus that he must expect to confront them.

This aspect of the mystery of redemption is at the very heart of mission. It is essentially through the battles of the spiritual life, through the battles of sanctity, that we contribute to the salvation of the world. There more than anywhere else, there more than in external activity, what is essential is fidelity to God in various vocations. In this sense, a contemplative who is faithful is infinitely more efficacious for the liberation of souls than an apostle who would engage in a lot of activity without an inward fidelity. Redemption is a mystery accomplished in the depths of the realm of souls, possessing mysterious laws and hidden communications. We know, because it is at the very heart of the mystery of Christ that spiritual effectiveness is, on this level, the supreme form of effectiveness.

III. Pointing toward the Resurrection

In the third place, St. Paul shows that all spiritual combat points toward the Resurrection, toward transfiguration and life. As he says in the Letter to the Romans (8:22), it is in a sense a giving birth that, through the labor pains, prepares for the blossoming of life. We can thus say that the apostle or the missionary consents to being put in the crucible because he knows that from this crucible will emerge a new creation. He thus accepts all of the difficulties, abandonment, and poverty that engagement in this mission will necessarily entail. All of this will enter into and disrupt his life. Moreover, what will cause the apostle the most suffering will be the feeling of impotence he will experience at times, when faced with obstacles and failures. All of this, offered in love, is the mystery of redemption, from which the Resurrection, fruitfulness, and life will spring. This is why St. Paul writes this extraordinary phrase: "We who live are continually given up to death for the sake of Jesus, so that the life of Jesus may be manifested in our mortal flesh; so death is at work in us and life in you" (2 Cor. 4:11-12).

Here we see a wonderful paradox: to the extent that the apostle accepts death, he becomes a source of life for others. "Give Christ to others and keep the cross for yourself," says Fr. Huvelin. There is a mysterious connection between the share of sacrifice we take in our own life and the fruitfulness of this sacrifice in the lives of others. Love requires sacrifice; but on the other hand, sacrifice is only justified by a greater abundance of life. This is precisely what the Resurrection is. Through this death, life emerges in greater abundance and gives every sacrifice and battle its ultimate justification. It is through this heavy and difficult process, taken up first by Christ and then by the apostles in their turn, that the body of Christ, destined for the Resurrection, is gradually built up.

This is an important lesson for us: love is serious; it does not consist in feelings or easy actions. Love occasionally immerses us inextricably in sadness and trial. But these obstacles and these trials are part of the very substance of the missionary life, and so they ought not to surprise us. A person who will have left for a Muslim country only to abandon it after a short period of time because he has discovered that a particular Muslim does not convert so easily, will have entirely misunderstood mission. For it is through this very obstacle, and through fidelity to love in this obstacle, that the love that never surrenders itself will always ultimately overcome. But this love will overcome at the end of an often long fidelity and a lot of patience — just like Christ, who was himself patient, who endured and suffered trials and failure. It is through fidelity that the love for our non-Christian sisters and brothers becomes authentic and ends by bearing fruit. Love that has not thus been tested is not yet entirely true and certain. If it is faithful, it will be rewarded, because love is always ultimately fruitful; it is always a source of resurrection.

In offering ourselves to the Lord for missionary service, we ask him to give us this serious and faithful love, a love that is capable of enduring trials and that is rooted so deeply in our hearts that it is not at the mercy of the ephemeral trials that will inevitably cross our paths. We ask that through these trials, our love will deepen, endure, and ultimately bear fruit.

CHAPTER THREE

The Mission of the Holy Spirit

We began this work with a discussion of the Holy Trinity, placing emphasis on the love of the Father. We then centered our meditation on Christ, his coming and his action. We will end by exploring how the Holy Spirit accomplishes the work of the Father and the Son in the Church.

I. "The River of Living Water Flowed from the Throne of God and the Lamb"

The remarkable theological vision that St. John describes in the book of Revelation (22:1-5) is that of the unfolding of the work of Christ and the Trinity in its final moment. Christ came to seek human nature. He assumed our flesh. At the Ascension, he brought it into the House of the Father, that is, into the Trinitarian life, and henceforward — this is the foundation for our hope — a part of us, a part of our flesh, is already immersed in the abyss of the Holy Trinity, because this is the flesh that Christ took on in Mary's womb. The Christian mystery is essentially the gesture of the Word of God assuming our flesh. The paradox of Christ is that he is fully God and fully flesh, and not some sort of intermediary who would be neither God nor flesh. The heretics of the early centuries had much difficulty understanding this teaching of Chalcedon. This affirmation is extraordinarily realistic: the flesh of Christ is my own; it is my humanity with all of its limitation, its slavishness, its smallness in everything that constitutes it.

This flesh did not succeed in raising itself up to the Trinity in spite of all the efforts of the various religions. These religions search for the Trinity, but they do not find it. This is why the Trinity came to search for the flesh, assumed it, and brought it into itself. Henceforward, the Father has given this flesh, brought into the Trinity by the Son, the gift of the Spirit. This is the moment that separates the Ascension from Pentecost, which St. Peter alludes to in his first speech to the Jews in the Acts of the Apostles (2:32-33): "God raised up this Jesus: of this we are all witnesses. And now, having been raised to the right hand of God and having received from the Father the promised Holy Spirit, he has poured forth what you see."

Here St. Peter puts what St. John says in another way: the Father gives the Spirit to the flesh to which the Son was united. He does not need to give it to the Son because the Son possesses the Spirit from all eternity. We ought especially to enjoy meditating on this beautiful moment of the life of the Trinity between the Ascension and Pentecost: that incredible moment of the eternal wedding of the Word of God and human nature wherein the Son brings his espoused flesh into the House of the Father, who pours forth the Spirit onto the Spouse, filling the Spouse with the Spirit. In a sense, a Pentecost occurs in the depths and abyss of the Trinity before the visible Pentecost: it is the Father's anointing of the Spouse within the hidden world of God.

Henceforward, the Spouse, the flesh, human nature, filled with the Spirit, pours forth the Spirit in its turn. The river of living water, which is the Spirit, is poured forth by the Lamb, as St. Peter said: "having received from the Father the promised Spirit, he poured forth what you see and hear" (Acts 2:33).

A glance at the fruits of the Spirit — he converts hearts, he heals the sick, he renews the Church — reveals a mysterious reality through which an undeniable presence emerges that is not of flesh and blood. What acts within this Church and within her sanctifying power, what constitutes the principle of her continuity and her infallibility, cannot be the people of flesh and blood that make her up: they are human like all others, and they demonstrate this all too often. Rather, it is the Spirit who shines through these people at certain moments. The Spirit alone is capable of working such wonders.

The life of the Spirit that fills the Spouse and penetrates human nature is ordered toward the communication of itself to every human nature. This is why at Pentecost the life of the Spirit, which is here compared to a river flowing from the throne of God and of the Lamb, pours forth and seeks to assume all of humanity. The river of living water is the Spirit working in the depths of the whole of humanity in order to bring it life. *Spiritus Domini replet orbem terrae* — this must be taken literally: "The Holy Spirit fills the universe." From the perspective of faith, all people bathe in this ocean of the Holy Spirit, but are penetrated by him in varying degrees. The Spirit takes advantage of the slightest movement of goodwill in the most humble soul and leads this soul gradually to open itself to him. Pre-evangelization is the Holy Spirit acting within the pagan soul that is particularly dear to him. We befriend this moment of the Spirit in which he has not yet accomplished his work; this period of beginnings and preparations is the moment of the Spirit that we make our own. We will have been a little of this Spirit with respect to Muslims, atheists, or Buddhists if, because of us, they become a little more open to the Holy Spirit. It is not up to us to convert, but to facilitate the work of the Spirit, and the Spirit converts when he wishes.

The Spirit makes use of us; we are his instruments. The Spirit is present and at work, and we can either help him or, on the contrary, become an obstacle to him. If we are not with the Spirit, we are against him, and this is something terrible. There is no neutrality. There are only witnesses and counterwitnesses. The Church is sometimes a counterwitness. Christians are sometimes counterwitnesses. Rather than facilitate the coming of the Church, they occasionally render it next to impossible when they present a face of the Church that can only repulse others, whether this be through a lack of love, or a lack of intelligence — intelligence being a fruit of the Spirit. This shows us how much we must ourselves be transparent and open to the Spirit, so that he can work through us. The Spirit is thus poured forth everywhere and seeks to assume all things. We must return to the essential image of the river of living water, which seeks to penetrate everything and collides with resistance, but which ultimately carries away this resistance and ends by bringing all things to the Father.

The Spirit is also represented by another biblical image: "I have come to set fire to the earth, and how I wish that it was already blazing" (Luke 12:49). The Spirit is also a tongue of fire: *"Fons vivus, ignis."* This is the heart of the paradox: the Spirit is a source both of living water and of fire. The hymn at Pentecost invites us to pass from one image to the other, so that we do not become enslaved by images; and it also shows us clearly that the Spirit represents all forms of power at once. He is the flame of souls, a flame that seeks to set all things on fire, to melt what is hardened, to bring to life what is dead. And he collides with resistances in people's hearts, with wood as hard as stone that does not allow itself to be set afire.

II. The Spirit Descends upon the City

The city is the world in which we live. The paradox continues here. Ours is a world of nuclear power, of great gatherings, of international organization through the U.N. or through UNESCO. It is the world of this particular humanity in which we live that bathes in the Holy Spirit. Our faith does not transport us into some fantastic universe.

For many people, religion is a sort of dream world juxtaposed to real life; it is opium, in the strict sense of the word, a little consolation we give ourselves in life. For some people, eternity represents a form of revenge against a life that has been for them a source of sorrow.

It is a compensation. Marx is right: religion is an opiate for some people.

But these ways of being Christian lack a hold on contemporary people, and the life of the Spirit is meaningless if it does not confront the reality in which we dwell. This is the very problem of the Church today. It is a matter of knowing how the Spirit is capable of assuming contemporary humanity, because it is the real world that the Spirit must penetrate, the world of modern civilization, the world of technology, of the town, of the city, of the expansion and the awakening of the peoples of the Third World with the resulting transformation for the idea of mission. It is the world with its own resistances, which are involuntary before becoming voluntary; in other words, resistances that are built into the very structures of things.

The creative work necessary for the Spirit and for us thus becomes greater. By what means do we engage this world so that it opens up to the spiritual element that it lacks? For this world the great temptation is being sufficient unto itself; through a form of collective pride, humanity claims to be capable of solving its problems on its own. There is something breathtakingly exciting about certain forms of scientific invention, about the journeys of astronauts; and all those things make up a sort of profane mythology. Nevertheless, it is precisely this world that we must engage and that the Spirit must appropriate. For this world needs the Spirit. In many respects, it calls out for the Spirit — that is, it is aware of its emptiness, of its incompleteness, its void, and its suffering.

One of the most impressive gifts in our day is the gesture of the world toward the Church — an extraordinary gesture, but one that may be frustrated, since the world's desire almost goes beyond the possibilities of the Church to fulfill it. By increasingly breaking out of routines, by penetrating to the heart of problems with the intelligence, by the boldness of creativity and the intensity of love, we can go quite far. But we may anxiously ask ourselves if the whole Church will follow; for before elevating the pagan world, the Spirit must first elevate the body of Christians, which is often the more difficult task.

It is only to the extent that the Spirit elevates Christian people, as John XXIII put it so well, that he will be able to reach the pagan world: the reform of the Church is the condition for the conversion of the world. This follows a rigorous logic. The Church must be permeated with the Spirit; she must renew herself and become alive with the life of the Spirit. When the Church is not alive, when the episcopate is not animated with a missionary zeal, when the priesthood is not sufficiently radiant with faith and with the Holy Spirit, when Christian people become what Maritain calls "the Christian world," that is, a sociological reality set up within Christianity, then the Church becomes an institution that hinders the Spirit.

The Spirit descends upon the city in order to reinvigorate within it the "trees of life," in other words — here, again, we have a paradox of images — in order to make the city a paradise. Heaven is not something beyond; it is the world itself when it is animated by the life of the Spirit. Heaven was formerly the spring of divine life in which the trees of life grew and flourished. Heaven is already the Church, as the Fathers of the Church have said. It is creation itself and thus this actual universe when, in the Holy Spirit, it attains to its ultimate fulfillment, its total fullness, when it is truly alive. Ultimately, the only thing we desire for the people of today is that they be fully alive. But we know that this can only be when they live in the Spirit. A person who does not live in the Spirit is dead, according to the language of the Bible. He or she lacks this participation in the life of God outside of which one cannot be truly alive.

This remarkable vision of the life of the Spirit coming from the Trinity, at work in the whole of humanity, is a missionary prayer, the contemplation of the sacred history not only of the past, but also of the present. A Christian is one who is aware of living in the midst of sacred history, at the same time that he or she lives in economic and political history. The dimension of faith and the prophetic vision (which is the same thing as missionary prayer) brings here something unique that non-Christians have a right to expect from us. It is the same thing Christ brings, calling forth from the very midst of the modern city the fruits of the Spirit; inspiring sanctity in the laity, in the clergy, and in the religious life; inspiring prayer as a complementary witness to work. For a world that would be nothing but a world of work and organization, a world that lacked prayer and contemplation, would be a sort of hell.

"The authentic city is one in which men have their homes and God has his," according to La Pira — one in which the monastery sits next to the factory, in which the factory worker is simultaneously a contemplative. Countless people work toward the edification of the scientific and organic city in the world. But this world risks losing its dimension of worship: it requires engineers who are at the same time people of adoration. In this respect, we must be relentless: the world could perish from lack of worship just as it could perish from lack of organization. Adoration is one of the constituent elements of a city. To speak of the missionary spirit, then, is not to speak of something exotic. It is to place ourselves at the very heart of the Spirit's growth in the society in which we live.

III. The Spirit's Action in Our Lives

The Word of God has poured the Spirit into the Church; in other words, the Spirit has not been communicated strictly individually. He is given to the Church; he is confided to the apostles so that they can communicate him. The order God has ordained is such that the Spirit communicates himself first to a group of people, and then, through them, to the following groups. It is thus through us that the Spirit communicates himself to others. But in order for the Spirit to pass through us, we must first be open to him; we must be docile; we must allow him to instruct us: "Only the Spirit of God sounds the depths of God" (1 Cor. 2:10). We cannot say "*Abba!* Father!" except in the Holy Spirit. The Spirit alone guides us to the Son and draws us to the Father. Indeed, "the Spirit bears witness with our spirit that we are sons of God" (Rom. 8:16). It is he who allows us to understand spiritual things: "the man of the flesh does not understand spiritual things" (Rom. 8:5); the Spirit alone allows us to taste them and to love them.

121

Praying means allowing the Spirit to instruct us: the Spirit allows us to understand and to taste the things of God. He gives us, in particular, an understanding of God's plan; he brings us into the ways of God. The Spirit gives us this important discernment, this gift of wisdom, which allows us to discern what is according to God's will in such a way as to bring it to bear on our practical decisions and to establish a hierarchy of values and order our occupations, not only according to human wisdom and prudence, but also according to the folly of the Cross and the inspiration of the Gospel.

The Holy Spirit allows us to feel the primacy of God's work, the primacy of mission, in which not all of us may participate wholly. This is a privileged vocation reserved only for some; but we must all recognize it as privileged. Christ asks most from those he loves most, and even if our vocations are not this one, we are obligated to recognize the grandeur of the missionary vocation. We must, through each of our vocations, retain the sense of the primacy of the inspiration from the Spirit and place the greatness of sanctity above the greatness of the mind and of the flesh. A tiny humble saint is infinitely greater than the greatest scientific inventions and the greatest artistic achievements. A respect for spiritual things and a just hierarchy of values are to be found here.

The Spirit gives us a sense of spiritual things, of their importance, and a capacity to discern them. This is what we must bear witness to, and we must be penetrated with these convictions ourselves in order to make them understood to those around us, as well as to justify certain decisions and commitments. If we sacrifice certain things with respect to the values of the mind or of the flesh or any other values, it is because, for us, the spiritual comes absolutely first in the hierarchy of values. If we do not bear witness to him in our lives, the Spirit, thus stifled, will no longer manifest himself. This witness, which appears in the saints, must also appear in us.

First, the Spirit is a Spirit of Understanding, who allows us to judge according to the Spirit, because decisions rest upon convictions. It is to the extent that we are convinced of a certain hierarchy that we will consider it natural to order our lives accordingly.

Secondly, the Spirit is a Spirit of Love — *"Fons vivus, ignis, caritas"* — who opens our hearts to the world's suffering, to the spiritual suffering of souls. He teaches us to love; he expands our hearts and brings us out of our selfishness and usual self-preoccupation. He raises us up from that which is small or petty in our concerns; he keeps us open to the calls that emerge from the world, even if we can respond to them only partially. He expands the spaces of charity, as St. Augustine said, and brings us into harmony with the heart of Christ, embracing in love and thus in prayer all of the needs of the world around us, especially the spiritual needs.

Finally, the Spirit is a Spirit of Strength. Without strength the other virtues would be nothing; strength is not a virtue, but it is what allows virtues truly to be virtues. We all have weak virtues: a little faith, a little love, a little hope. But only strong virtues are serious and effective. Love is as strong as death. Our charity often recoils before its realizations because of timidity or cowardice. True charity works, acts, accomplishes, and fulfills. Because it is realistic, it is infinitely humble. When we exercise charity, we are aware that we must often be content with small results. Authentic charity is full of tact, because it is too mindful of fulfillment to commit indiscretions or premature actions. It is like the gardener who surveys the growth of a plant, always careful not to force its development prematurely.

The virtue of time, of patience, is essential, not only insofar as it waits and endures, but also insofar as it acts in time respecting the law of time, and knowing how to take account of opportune moments. Such is the tact and the justice of authentic charity. Precipitation denotes a lack of openness to the Holy Spirit insofar as it is a will to bring to an end, to work things out, while the Holy Spirit works in the depths, in slowness, and in time.

We invoke the Holy Spirit for each one of us: may he enlighten us, strengthen us, and help us to love, because we all need to be healed. We invoke him above all so that he may give us love. We also invoke him for the whole of the Church. We feel intensely today the world's expectation and the Church's immense responsibility.

May the Holy Spirit enlighten the Supreme Pontiff and his bishops; may the Church truly be renewed in the Spirit of the Spouse with whom the Word of God has united himself and who continues to exist in the world today. May the Father always fill the Church with the Spirit so that, renewed thus in the Spirit, she can bring to people and to the world of our generation the life of the Spirit outside of whom there can be nothing but spiritual death, and without whom there can be no fulfillment.